THE U.S. CONSTITUTION

AN OWNER'S MANUAL

by Stuart Matranga

New York, New York

The publisher wishes to recognize
Samantha Tesser Haimo for her
dedication to the law and for
helping to make this book possible.

This book is dedicated to all those who have served,
past and present, to defend our Constitution, our freedom,
and the rights and liberties of all Americans.

Designed by Karen Viola

The U.S. Constitution: An Owner's Manual
Copyright © 2019 Midgard Education Publishing, LLC
All rights reserved under International and Pan-American
Copyright Conventions. This book may not be reproduced in whole
or in part in any form without written permission of the publisher.

Printed in the United States of America

ISBN: 978-1-7337050-3-5

MIDGARD

EDUCATION PUBLISHING, LLC

Bruce A. Bernstein, Chairman
Jay Gissen, Chief Executive Officer
Stuart Matranga, Editor-in-Chief

midgardeducation.com
contact us at:
info@midgardeducation.com

Welcome!

Congratulations! You are the proud owner of a shiny new nation. It comes with no guarantees. It costs you more than you can imagine—not just money, but also occasionally blood. It's designed to work imperfectly and needs the constant attention of highly skilled mechanics to service, repair, and sometimes replace parts.

But it's yours. You own it. So let's see what you bought into.

CONTENTS:

"The Constitution is the guide which I will never abandon."
—George Washington

"Our new Constitution is now established. Everything seems to promise it will be durable; but, in this world, nothing is certain except death and taxes."
—Ben Franklin

"An inviolable respect for the Constitution is the vital principle, the sustaining energy of a free government."
—Alexander Hamilton

"I sincerely rejoice at the acceptance of our new Constitution. It is a good canvas on which some strokes only want retouching."
—Thomas Jefferson

"We have no government, armed with power, capable of contending with human passions, unbridled by morality and religion. Avarice, ambition, revenge and licentiousness would break the strongest cords of our Constitution, as a whale goes through a net."
—John Adams

"The language of our Constitution is already undergoing interpretations unknown to its founders."
—James Madison

SETTING UP

First of all, a lot of people get confused by the advertising, so let's be clear about the difference between the Declaration of Independence and the United States Constitution.

Making a Declaration

The Declaration of Independence was written in Philadelphia in July of 1776 mostly by Thomas Jefferson but with able assists from Benjamin Franklin and John Adams. Its purpose was to annoy the British overlords of America, to be the mission statement for a new nation that did not yet exist, and to put the blame for the Revolution on the British criminal conspiracy to oppress the colonists. It includes Enlightenment ideas about liberty, equality, and justice, as well as happiness. It's just about the most radical document produced in the history of forever because, well, read some of it for yourself:

THE DECLARATION OF INDEPENDENCE

What It Says

When in the Course of human events, it becomes necessary for one people to dissolve the political bands which have connected them with another, and to assume among the powers of the earth, the separate and equal station to which the Laws of Nature and of Nature's God entitle them, a decent respect to the opinions of mankind requires that they should declare the causes which impel them to the separation.

We hold these truths to be self-evident, that all men are created equal, that they are endowed by their Creator with certain unalienable Rights, that among these are Life, Liberty and the pursuit of Happiness.

Governments are instituted among Men deriving their just powers from the consent of the governed.

What It Means

We are now going to tell the world why we want to go our own way by detailing our reasons.

Obviously, all men are born with the same rights to live free and happy.
Note: They mean white men. Not women. Not African Americans—slaves or free. Not Native Americans.
Also note: The pursuit of happiness (financial satisfaction) is easier to promise than property, which had been originally written.

Governments are made by men to protect those rights.
This is a game changer in the world. People forming their own government was basically unprecedented. Although no government has been formed yet—that's where the Constitution comes in.

That whenever any Form of Government becomes destructive of these ends, it is the Right of the People to alter or to abolish it, and to institute new Government, laying its foundation on such principles and organizing its powers in such form, as to them shall seem most likely to effect their Safety and Happiness.

Prudence, indeed, will dictate that Governments long established should not be changed for light and transient causes; and accordingly all experience hath shewn, that mankind are more disposed to suffer, while evils are sufferable, than to right themselves by abolishing the forms to which they are accustomed.

But when a long train of abuses and usurpations, pursuing invariably the same Object evinces a design to reduce them under absolute Despotism, it is their right, it is their duty, to throw off such Government, and to provide new Guards for their future security. Such has been the patient sufferance of these Colonies; and such is now the necessity which constrains them to alter their former Systems of Government.

If the people don't like the government, they can change it. No one else has a higher authority than the people.

They write as if this is standard operating procedure when, in fact, overturning an established government has hardly ever been tried, and never to put power in the hands of the people.

Changing governments is a big deal, and only with good reason should people rise out of comfortable habits and rebel against their government.

We have good reasons to rebel against a tyrant. We must do this now. We can't take it anymore, yo.

The history of the present King of Great Britain is a history of repeated injuries and usurpations, all having in direct object the establishment of an absolute Tyranny over these States. To prove this, let Facts be submitted to a candid world.

We accuse King George III of tyranny and we'll list his crimes now. (Notice the use of "States" instead of "Colonies." In the mind of the Founders, the divorce has already happened.)

What follows in the Declaration is a list of twenty-seven grievances ranging from the king's refusal to acknowledge laws to bunking soldiers in people's private homes to controlling trade with other nations. ("He has abdicated Government here by declaring us out of his Protection and waging War against us. He has plundered our seas, ravaged our coasts, burnt our towns, and destroyed the lives of our people.") But it's the twenty-eighth grievance, the one the Founders had to take out at the last minute in order to get the Southern states to sign, that resulted in the inevitable Civil War less than a hundred years later.

The Edited-Out Grievance:

He [the king] has waged cruel war against human nature itself, violating its most sacred rights of life and liberty in the persons of a distant people who never offended him, captivating & carrying them into slavery in another hemisphere or to incur miserable death in their transportation thither. This piratical warfare, the opprobrium of infidel powers, is the warfare of the Christian King of Great Britain. Determined to keep open a market where Men should be bought & sold, he has prostituted his negative for suppressing every legislative attempt to prohibit or restrain this execrable commerce. And that this assemblage of horrors might want no fact of distinguished die, he is now exciting those very people to rise in arms among us, and to purchase that liberty of which he has deprived them, by murdering the people on whom he has obtruded them: thus paying off former crimes committed against the Liberties of one people with crimes which he urges them to commit against the lives of another.

The Southern states opposed this clause attacking slavery and threatened to break away from the Northern states, who supported it, if this clause remained in the Declaration. That Jefferson was himself a slaveholding Southerner made no difference. His fellow Virginians thought he was a traitor and intended to ruin him. Jefferson deleted the clause and hoped the next generation would end slavery. They didn't. There was an attempt during the Constitutional Convention ten years later to end slavery, but that failed too. Until 1865 millions of people continued to live in bondage and the nation broke apart during the four years of the Civil War, resulting in the deaths of over 600,000 Americans.

TAKEAWAY

The Declaration of Independence asserts that there is such a thing as the United States, but it does not define it or explain it in any detail. That will come with the Constitution eleven years later.

The Declaration ends with a bold warning.

We, therefore, the Representatives of the united States of America, in General Congress, Assembled, appealing to the Supreme Judge of the world for the rectitude of our intentions, do, in the Name, and by Authority of the good People of these Colonies, solemnly publish and declare, That these united Colonies are, and of Right ought to be Free and Independent States, that they are Absolved from all Allegiance to the British Crown, and that all political connection between them and the State of Great Britain, is and ought to be totally dissolved; and that as Free and Independent States, they have full Power to levy War, conclude Peace, contract Alliances, establish Commerce, and to do all other Acts and Things which Independent States may of right do. — And for the support of this Declaration, with a firm reliance on the protection of Divine Providence, we mutually pledge to each other our Lives, our Fortunes, and our sacred Honor.

We're all in. Let the world know that we are now in open rebellion against Great Britain and we know that if we lose we will all be killed as traitors, but this fight for freedom is worth the risk.

Customer Support

Fill in this graphic organizer about the Declaration of Independence.

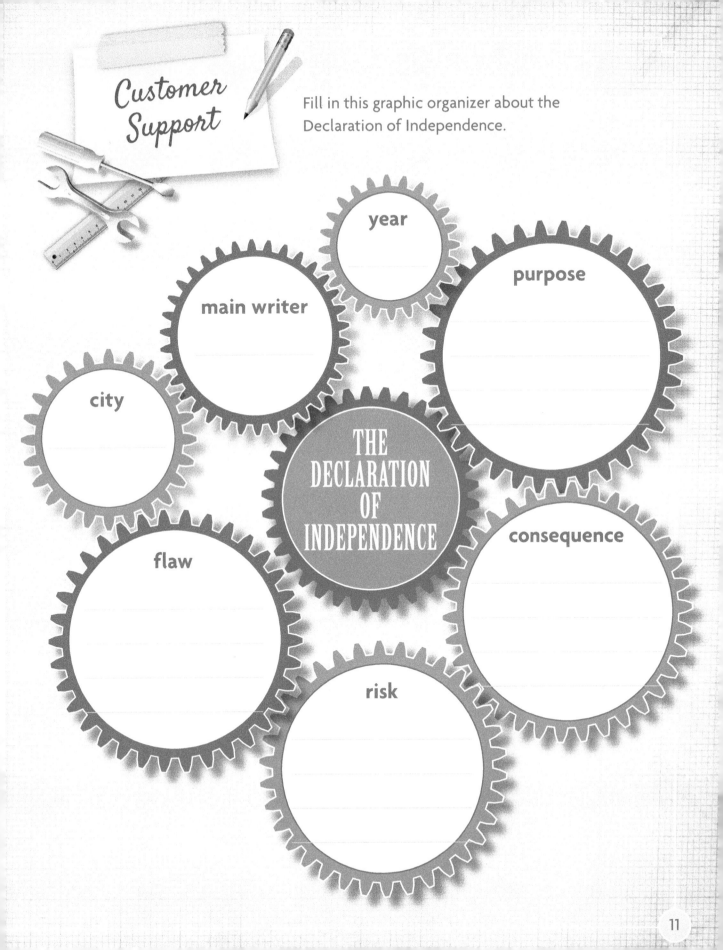

year

main writer

purpose

city

THE
DECLARATION
OF
INDEPENDENCE

consequence

flaw

risk

GETTING STARTED

Previous prototypes of the brand of government you now live in go way back. The U.S. Constitution became the most influential political document in the history of the world, changing not only the United States, but how government is conceived of in many parts of the world. But it didn't come from nowhere. There was a whole lot of beta testing that came before.

Hammurabi's Code

One of the first launches happened when the Babylonian emperor Hammurabi, wearing his customary black turtleneck, introduced his exciting new code to second millennials (BCE).

We'll spare you the gruesome details—the eye for an eye, tooth for a tooth forms of punishments that fit the crime (called *lex talionis*)—but Hammurabi wrote laws to protect women, slaves, and workers. He set up judges and required that witnesses testify openly. The code included concepts such as innocent until proven guilty and strict restrictions on fake news (or what we once called lying). If you're going to accuse someone, especially of a major crime, you better have evidence or you'll end up in the trash folder.

TAKEAWAY

Hammurabi established laws "to bring about the rule of righteousness in the land, to destroy the wicked and the evildoers; so that the strong should not harm the weak, to further the well-being of mankind."

Customer Support

Make up three modern-day laws in the spirit of *lex talionis*.

1.

2.

3.

Athenian Democracy

When Pericles became CEO of Athens in 461 BCE, he expanded on the relatively new concept of democracy. He made sure common workers participated in assemblies that created laws.

The word *democracy* comes from *demos*, meaning "all citizens," and *kratos*, meaning "to rule." Athenian direct democracy required 30,000–60,000 citizens (men who owned property) to assemble on a hillside one to three times per month. They voted on specific issues, such as whom to go to war with, whom to appoint as judges, whether to send a peace offer to Persia, or whether to kill Socrates. Before the innovation of hand-raising, they voted by placing black or white pebbles in urns and doing a lot of counting. The word for *ballot* comes from the French word for *ball*, to approximate how the ancient Greeks voted.

For the sake of convenience, they also had a council of about five hundred citizens who decided what issues would be up for a vote in the assembly. Council members served for one-year terms—no more than two years in a row.

An even smaller group, an executive committee of about fifty, met in the agora, the open marketplace, to discuss major issues and suggest voting topics to the council.

Another layer of government, the law courts with 6,000 elected jurors, actually wrote out proposed laws or reviewed current ones.

The biggest problem with the Greek system was that the most educated, meaning the richest, people tended to hog power. Also, a persuasive speaker could sway the mob to vote for a special interest.

TAKEAWAY

Democracy depends on complexity. The checks and balances on different parts of government prevent—or at least slow down— any one person from getting too powerful.

Customer Support

Define these other types of government in ancient Greece.

Monarchy:

Aristocracy:

Oligarchy:

Rome Rules

There is a lot to admire about the Roman Republic before it became an empire. The Romans developed what would become the Twelve Tablets of the Law.

These laws covered procedures for going to court. For example, if a man was summoned to court and he didn't show up, an officer would go to his house and call for him "loudly" every third day.

Other laws included conditions for paying back debts, the rights of fathers as heads of families, land rights, inheritance rights, the difference between committing a crime by day or at night (worse at night because it's sneaky to lurk about in the dark), how long to mourn, whom to marry and how to divorce, and the always popular "a person found guilty of lying shall be hurled down from the Tarpeian Rock."

More importantly than the laws themselves, the Romans created lawyers. They applied a scientific scrutiny to crime, punishment, law, and the process of jurisprudence (the legal system).

Roman Republican government, starting in 509 BCE, developed a complex web of bureaucracy that distributed power fairly and efficiently for about five hundred years.

The government consisted of two consuls, serving for one year each. They had to both agree on every law or they could veto each other—rule each other out. They could be replaced in emergencies by a temporary dictator. Several hundred senators (literally, "old men") came from the patrician or wealthier class, but only advised the consuls. They did not make laws or declare war. Assemblies were elected by plebeians, or common people, and formed in different blocks (military, religious, tribal, etc.) and actually made the laws, declared war, made peace treaties, and presided over major trials. There was also a judicial branch of magistrates to evaluate the laws and how they apply to specific cases.

TAKEAWAY

Most of the world's legal concepts come from Rome, and many legal terms come from the Roman language of Latin.

Some Common Latin Legal Terms

LATIN	ENGLISH
Alias	Another name
Alibi	At another place
Bona fide	In good faith
Cui bono	Who benefits?
Habeas corpus	Bring a person before the court
In loco parentis	In place of a parent
Modus operandi	Method of operating
Status quo	How things are
Quid pro quo	This for that
Verbatim	Word for word
Vice versa	The other way around

Customer
Support

Define these legal phrases.

Amicus curiae:

Caveat emptor:

Ipso facto:

Nolo contendere:

Sui generis:

The Social Contract

While Europeans were taking their first yawning steps out of the Middle Ages and into the Renaissance, reviving the spirit of Greek and Roman culture, they began to discover themselves as human individuals, not just subjects to kings and priests.

At the time of Leonardo da Vinci, early sixteenth-century Italy, Niccolò Machiavelli suggested in his book *The Prince* that people are mostly "thoughtless, gullible, manipulative, ungrateful, and unreliable; they lie, they fake, they are greedy for cash, and they melt away in the face of danger." In order to rule this rabble, he said, "it is better to be loved than feared, but it is much safer to be feared than loved."

Thomas Hobbes in early seventeenth-century England would agree. In his book *The Leviathan*, referring to the monstrosity of government, he argues that men need strict government, or they will resort to their "natural" life, which he describes with dystopian relish as "solitary, poor, nasty, brutish, and short."

At the end of that century, John Locke wrote *Two Treatises of Government*, agreeing and disagreeing with Hobbes. According to Locke, people can thrive if they have the right government to protect their "natural rights to life, liberty, and property." If the government attacks those rights, the government must be overthrown.

Across the channel in France a few years later, Charles Montesquieu wrote in *The Spirit of Laws* that man in nature is controlled by fear of not eating or of being eaten. "As soon as man enters into a state of society," he said, "he loses the sense of his weakness." He believed good governments controlled the worst impulses of humans.

All of these thoughts swirled in the mind of Jean-Jacques Rousseau. In 1762, he wrote *The Social Contract* and put a fine point on the argument in its first lines: "Man is born free, and everywhere he is in chains. One man thinks himself the master of others but remains more of a slave than they are." Rousseau said that a government that requires people to give up some liberty for security is a fake-out devised by the rich to keep everyone else in line. The social contract requires an "all for one, one for all" attitude where everyone equally participates in a pure democracy.

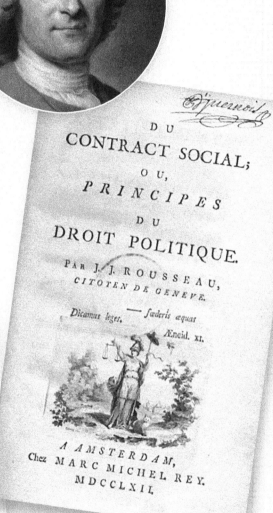

When Rousseau's book came out, Voltaire, the satirist and Rousseau's longtime frenemy, wrote to him: "I have received your new book against the human race and thank you for it. Never was such cleverness used in the design of making us all stupid."

TAKEAWAY

Enlightenment thinkers believed that, while individuals might have the right to control their own destiny, you can't trust people. Enlightenment ideas were very much on the minds of the Founders when they sat down to write the Constitution.

Match the philosopher with the one-word description.

Machiavelli		Humanism
Hobbes		Sarcasm
Locke		Cynicism
Montesquieu		Pessimism
Rousseau		Optimism
Voltaire		Idealism

The Great Binding Law

For centuries, several tribes in northeastern America had learned to live in peace under one government. The warring factions buried their weapons under the Great Tree of Peace and created the Iroquois Confederacy consisting of five tribes: the Mohawk, Cayuga, Oneida, Seneca, and Onondaga (later joined by the Tuscarora). They called themselves the Haudenosaunee after their essential mission, "People Building a Long House." The long house was symbolic of the community. Their government formed around the Great Binding Law, which drew the admiration of Benjamin Franklin and other

Founders as a practical model for their proposed American government.

The foundation of the law had three principles. *Righteousness* meant that everybody was treated with equity, according to their abilities and needs. *Health* included the mind, body, and spirit, all of which are strongest when there is peace among individuals and communities. *Justice* came from the equality of different people and the balance of each person's mind, body, and spirit. All 117 articles in the Iroquois Constitution are meant to promote those values.

Under this set of detailed laws, the elder women of each tribe selected representatives to meet in a council. The council debated matters such as war and peace. Their symbol was five (then six) arrows bundled together because one arrow can be cracked, but several together could not be. This, with thirteen arrows to represent the thirteen colonies, became part of the Great Seal of the United States.

Issues were debated by an "Older House," the Mohawk and Seneca, who then passed their decisions to the "Younger House" of Cayuga and Oneida. Tied votes would be decided by the Onondaga, but their ruling could be vetoed by either of the other houses.

Regular reports of the Grand Council's proceeding were printed in Franklin's newspapers as early as 1736.

Even more than this model of bicameral legislature (*bi* means "two" and *cameral* means "houses") to separate powers and to provide checks and balances on those in power, the Great Binding Law had provisions for individual human rights that went far beyond the Enlightenment thinkers and directly influenced the Bill of Rights that followed the Constitution. Among the rights listed were freedom of speech and the freedom of religion. The Iroquois ensured that women had a voice in the government. Their judicial court consisted mostly of a Women's Council to evaluate laws and to prescribe justice.

TAKEAWAY

The Founders admired and consulted with Native American leaders in the early days of the American government. The Iroquois influenced the structure of the U.S. government and its protections for freedom of expression.

Customer Support

Describe how you demonstrate the three principles of the Iroquois in your life.

Righteousness:

Health:

Justice:

The Albany Plan

In 1754, as the English and French did battle in North America (and all around the globe in what should be called the first world war but is known as the French and Indian or Seven Years' War), Benjamin Franklin left Philadelphia and went to Albany, New York, to meet the sachem, or chief, of the Mohawk nation, Hendrick Theyanoguin. Franklin wanted this moment, in the midst of the war between the English and French, to launch a new nation, America. He already knew that the Iroquois had an effective and powerful alliance. His intention, contrary to the aims of the British and most of the colonial representatives, was to model a new American government directly on the Iroquois template. His Albany Plan came right out of the Great Binding Law. It includes the formation of a Grand Council with representatives from each colony. It failed because

1) a United Colonies of America was seen as a threat to the British, and

2) the colonies did not want to compromise their authority by sharing power.

TAKEAWAY

Though his plan failed, Franklin made an independent America conceivable. The Iroquois advised the Continental Congress in 1776 and the Constitutional Convention in 1787.

Research and comment on the accuracy of this meme:

The U.S. Constitution's notion of democracy owes a lot to the Iroquois Tribes, including freedom of religion, freedom of speech, and separation of powers in government.

A big difference is, the Iroquois included women and non-whites.

Constitution: Version 1.0

In the midst of the Revolutionary War, the Continental Congress drafted the Articles of Confederation in November of 1777. It had to and did get ratified by all thirteen states in March of 1781.

There was a lot wrong with it. For one, it, well, read it for yourself.

The Articles of Confederation

Paraphrased from "The articles of Confederation and perpetual Union between the States of New Hampshire, Massachusetts-bay, Rhode Island and Providence Plantations, Connecticut, New York, New Jersey, Pennsylvania, Delaware, Maryland, Virginia, North Carolina, South Carolina, and Georgia."

• **Article I**. The Stile [name] of this confederacy shall be, "The United States of America."

• **Article II**. Each state retains all its rights, and every Power not by this expressly delegated to the United States.

• **Article III**. The states enter into a firm league of friendship with each other, for their common defense, security, Liberties, and their mutual and general welfare.

• **Article IV**. The free inhabitants of each state (except for beggars, vagabonds, and fugitives) shall be entitled to come and go freely to all the other states and be subject to that state's rights, laws, and taxes. Each state must respect the laws of all the other states.

• **Article V**. Each state shall send between no more than seven and no fewer than two delegates to Congress every year. Each delegate has one vote in Congress.

- **Article VI**. No State, without the Consent of the united States, can negotiate separate deals with foreign nations. No state can enter any treaties among each other without the consent of the united states. No state may impose taxes that interfere with existing treaties. No state can keep a standing army or navy, except each state can keep a well-regulated militia. No state can engage in war without the consent of the united States, except in wars with Indians.

- **Article VII**. In times of war, all officers from each state above the rank of colonel will be appointed by the united States' Congress.

- **Article VIII**. Costs of war or national expenses will be paid by each state into a treasury in proportion to the value of land in that state.

- **Article IX**. The powers of the united States' Congress are these; to wage war; to conduct treaties; to settle disputes among States; to regulate currency; to establish post offices; to make a budget. Congress needs the consent of at least nine states to act on any of these matters.

- **Article X**. When Congress is not in session, an executive committee may be given any of these powers as long as they act with the consent of at least nine states.

- **Article XI**. Canada is free to join this union, but any other colony may only join with the agreement of at least nine states.

- **Article XII**. All debts contracted by congress shall be charged to the united States for payment.

- **Article XIII**. Every State shall comply to the laws of the united states. No changes can be made to these articles unless Congress and every state legislature agrees to the changes.

Sounds okay until you realize that the framers forgot the *United* part of the United States. (Notice how even the word "united" is in lower case.) At this point, Americans are still thinking of their new nation as separate *states*. The new nation is usually referred to as a plural noun: the United States *are* a wild and crazy country, not the United States *is* a wild and crazy country.

What were the problems with the Articles? Well:

Why Did the Articles of Confederation Fail to Confederate?

1. It created a very weak central government with no details for how it was to govern, no process for governing, no executive to manage things, and no judicial system to review laws.

2. Nine out of thirteen states had to agree to pass new laws. That's almost 70 percent. That's a lot of agreement among delegates who had very different interests. What does Massachusetts know about the Carolina cotton trade? What does Georgia know about Connecticut fishing rights? Every law becomes a tough sell.

3. To change any law, it took 100 percent agreement among all the states.

4. The states had to pay the federal government basically whatever they wanted in taxes. There was no budget for an army or to build interstate roads or even to print federal currency.

5. Congress had no power to enforce their own laws.

6. Each state was free to print its own currency, as was the federal government, creating confusion where it hurt the most, in trade.

7. There was no plan to pay back the considerable debts from the Revolutionary War.

TAKEAWAY

The Articles of Confederation attempted to give each state autonomy while creating a unified government but failed at both.

Customer Support

Explain why you think each of these groups would want to change the Articles of Confederation.

Rich landowners:

Merchants:

Farmers:

Slaves:

The major players of the Revolution left the playing field in a confused jumble at the end of the war. Thomas Jefferson went to France to grieve for his dead wife and help instigate the French Revolution while serving as the American ambassador. John Adams had the thankless job of being the American representative to the English Court, where he was routinely mocked and bullied. Benjamin Franklin continued gallivanting around Europe while trying to get European banks to forgive at least some of the American debt. Alexander Hamilton returned to his law practice in New York. George Washington retired to his estate in Mount Vernon, Virginia.

While they weren't looking, a new revolution was about to start, and it almost put an end to the American experiment.

Shays' Rebellion

Everybody knows the United States was founded after a revolution. What many do not realize is that it was really founded after a rebellion. The Revolution broke Britain's control over the colonies and allowed a new nation to form. That nation, however, was disorganized, inefficient, and doomed to fail—as most leaders in Europe expected.

But in 1786, highly decorated Revolutionary War veteran Captain Daniel Shays faced bankruptcy in Massachusetts. The fledgling state government could not pay his minimal wages from the war, and Massachusetts claimed he owed taxes on his farm land, which earned no money during the war. He was in worse shape under the United States than he had been under the United Kingdom. And he was not alone.

Hundreds of other veterans joined Shays in front of the courthouse in Springfield demanding that the banks not foreclose on their farms, that the government pay them the money owed to them for fighting in the war, and that they be given more time to pay off their debts.

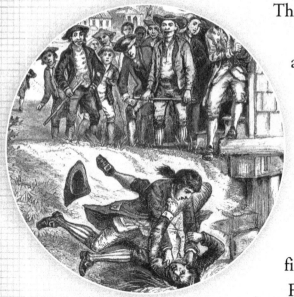

The government refused their requests.

Shays and the rebels became an army. They attacked the Massachusetts armory to get weapons and start an all-out insurrection.

Ironically, Massachusetts couldn't afford to pay for an army to stop Shays. A private army was enlisted, paid for by local merchants and bankers who would lose money if the farmers defaulted on their loans. The army chased off the rebels and pursued them for several weeks, finally capturing the leaders during a blizzard.

Four thousand rebels were pardoned, but Shays and a few other leaders were sentenced to be hanged.

The Founders who started the Revolution were mostly against Shays, claiming the ex-soldiers were ungrateful. Thomas Jefferson, though, supported them, writing to Abigail Adams, "I like a little rebellion now and then. The tree of liberty must be refreshed from time to time with the blood of patriots and tyrants. It is its natural manure."

Jefferson made his point to the retired but always influential George Washington. The general wrote to the people of Massachusetts, "I am mortified beyond expression when I view the clouds that have spread over the brightest morn that ever dawned upon any country. My humble opinion is to know precisely what the rebel farmers aim at. If they have real grievances, take care of them if possible."

Shays was pardoned. Massachusetts suspended the farmers' debts and reduced their taxes. A clear victory. But even more importantly, James Madison, a protégé of Jefferson, realized that the new nation was exposed to dangers from incidents they could not control. There was no general policy for states or individuals to discuss and decide on their disagreements under the Articles of the Confederation. He persuaded George Washington to come out of retirement and relaunch the United States with a new operating system called the Constitution.

TAKEAWAY

Shays' Rebellion saved the United States by forcing the government to reinvent itself.

Customer Support

Give one reason each to be for or against Shays' Rebellion.

I think Shays' Rebellion was right because

I think Shays' Rebellion was wrong because

Before we get to the Constitution basics, let's compare it to the systems that came before.

Governments That Influenced the Constitution

	Ancient Rome	Modern English	Old Iroquois	Articles of Confederation	TODAY'S CONSTITUTIONAL GOVERNMENT
Legislative	Senate 300–1,000, life terms, advises the Consuls Assemblies—groups of citizens, makes laws	Parliament House of Lords—750, most have life terms, 96 inherited, advises only House of Commons—650, 5-year terms, makes laws, policies	Grand Council Elder Brothers—31 Mohawk, Seneca Younger Brothers—19 Cayuga, Oneida Spiritual and practical guidance, voted by Clan Mothers	Congress 1 representative from each state, term and election determined by state. 9/13 votes to approve laws No power to tax or make binding policies	Congress Senate—100 members, 6-year terms, makes laws, policies House—435 members, 2-year terms, makes laws
Executive	2 Consuls—1-year terms, lead army, manage government	Monarch—inherited, advises only Prime Minister—elected, manages government	Onondaga Fire Keepers, call meetings, decide topics, break ties	President—presides over Congress, advises only	President—4-year terms, leads army, manages government
Judicial	8 Judges—1-year terms, appointed by Assemblies	12 Supreme Court Judges—retire by 70, review laws Lower courts	Determined by clans and tribes, usually female led	No federal courts Arbitration process	Supreme Court justices—currently 9, life terms, appointed by president, review laws Lower courts
Local	Magistrates—life-terms, rule on legal disputes	Divided into four kingdoms, several regions, councils, districts, parishes	Clans formed from family groups, led by oldest woman, who appoints leaders and Council representatives	States have autonomy and authority over federal government	State governors—4-year terms State assemblies—2-year terms Several county and city municipalities
Individual	Twelve Tablets of Law	Bill of Rights of 1689	Great Binding Law	States' Bills of Rights	Bill of Rights, amendments

In 1787, with John Adams and Thomas Jefferson absent, James Madison and Alexander Hamilton tried to convince Americans why they needed a reboot. They, along with John Jay, wrote a series of pamphlets called *The Federalist Papers* that explained exactly why a new Constitution was needed.

The Federalists vs. the Anti-Federalists

The eighty-five pamphlets of *The Federalist Papers* are marvelously brilliant for the eighteenth century, but they are somewhat difficult to get through for modern audiences. If you feel brave, go ahead and look them up for a deeper reading. Alexander Hamilton and John Adams were strong Federalists, while James Madison and George Washington were somewhat on the fence. Federalists were afraid of the mob. They feared democracy where common people could be easily persuaded by a charismatic speaker and that they would have too much say in government. They believed in a ruling class of well-educated (wealthy) men to run a strong central government. Still, they wanted a system of checks and balances. The Congress, the president, and the Supreme Court (the three branches of government) keep watch on each other to keep the different parts of government honest.

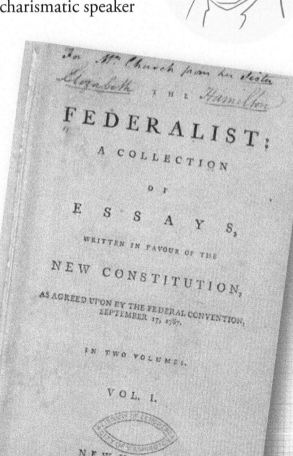

Then, of course, there were *The Anti-Federalist Papers*. You can look them up, too, though they're even more dense to read. These essays were compiled by several authors including Patrick Henry (the "Give me liberty or give me death" guy) and Mercy Otis Warren (a female Founding "Father"), and influenced long-distance from Paris by Thomas Jefferson. The Anti-Federalists feared the inevitable rise of tyranny because power corrupts even the most idealistic leaders. They believed in representatives drawn from all parts of society, including workers, farmers, and the uneducated, to run strong local governments. They wanted a weakened central government to manage things but insisted on a bill of rights to protect individuals from the central and local governments. Basically, they believed in what became known as "Jeffersonian democracy," small governments made up of local people who know best how to rule themselves.

TAKEAWAY

The United States is the product of two contrasting philosophies, Federalism (strong central government) and Anti-Federalism (strong local governments).

Customer Support

Identify the following quotes as being Federalist (F) or Anti-Federalist (AF).

1. "If men were angels, no government would be necessary. In framing a government which is to be administered by men over men, the great difficulty lies in this: you must first enable the government to control the governed; and in the next place oblige it to control itself."

2. "I had rather be a free citizen of the small republic of Massachusetts, than an oppressed subject of the great American empire."

3. "It is to be lamented that the designing under the pretense of having discovered a panacea for all the ills of the people, are establishing a system of government that will prove more destructive than the wooden horse filled with soldiers to the city of Troy."

4. "Nothing is more certain than the necessity of government, and it is equally undeniable, that whenever and however it is instituted, the people must cede to it some of their natural rights in order to vest it with requisite powers."

5. "The great will struggle for power, honor and wealth; the poor become a prey to avarice, insolence and oppression."

6. "Safety from external danger is the most powerful director of national conduct. Even the ardent love of liberty will, after a time, give way to its dictates. To be more safe, people at length become willing to run the risk of being less free."

Answers on page 160

Jefferson vs. Hamilton

Perhaps the most famous, fundamental, articulate, and ongoing disagreement about the Constitution occurred before, during, and after it was created. Thomas Jefferson and Alexander Hamilton nearly came to blows when they were in the same room. If they didn't draw each other's blood, they did draw each other's ink in a series of sometimes anonymous letters, speeches, and edicts. Both men, both confidants and "sons" to Washington, saw the world from different and unexpected points of view.

Jefferson, the entitled, land-owning aristocrat, believed in the common man. Hamilton, who started in America as an immigrant, believed in an aristocracy of merit and wealth. Jefferson had slaves but hated having them. Hamilton, who very possibly had an African ancestor, abhorred slavery. Jefferson, an introvert, believed in the quiet, country life, and was a compulsive inventor. Hamilton, an extrovert, loved the bustle of the city and almost single-handedly created Wall Street in New York as the financial center of the world. Jefferson was a Francophile. Hamilton favored the English. Both men served in Washington's first cabinet, Jefferson as secretary of state, Hamilton as secretary of the treasury.

By the efforts of their mutual friend James Madison, the true architect and major writer of the Constitution and the mediator and "adult in the room" during their contentious meetings, they were able to work together to continue the spirit of compromise that is written into the Constitution.

Their creative friction played a big part in the early days of the United States and determined, among other things, the location of the new federal city (Washington, D.C.), the creation of American banks, and our political system. Hamilton started the Federalist Party and Jefferson, just to confuse middle school students for the rest of time, started the Democratic-Republicans.

TAKEAWAY

After Hamilton was murdered by Aaron Burr, Jefferson had a statue of Hamilton placed inside his home in Monticello. They needed each other, and the nation needed both of them.

Customer Support

Jefferson-Hamilton Venn Diagram

Fill in what Jefferson and Hamilton have in common.

JEFFERSON
- small federal government
- all white males vote
- strict Constitution
- individual rights

HAMILTON
- big federal government
- rich white males vote
- loose Constitution
- anti-states rights

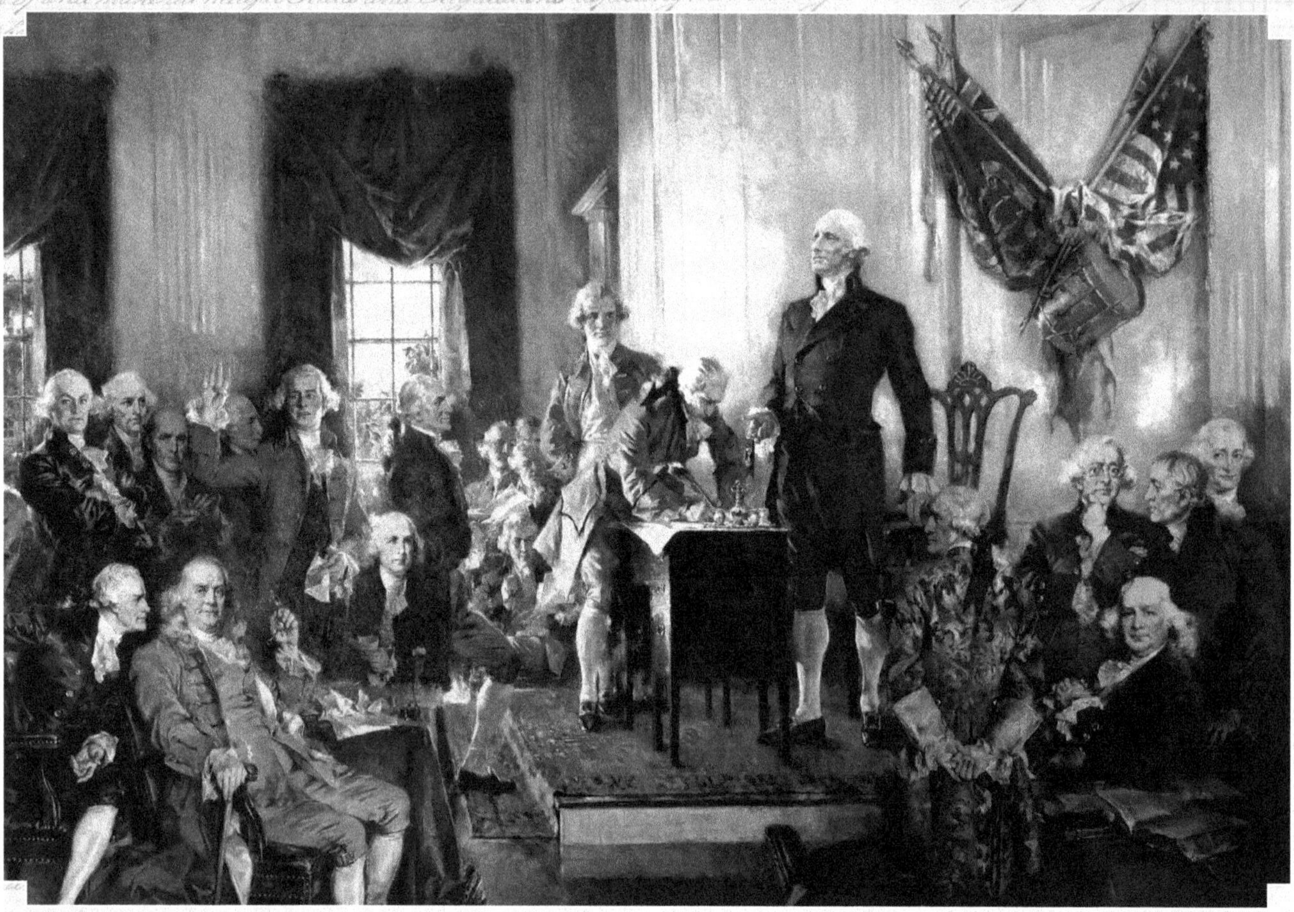

The Constitutional Convention

From May to September of 1787, each state sent delegates to Philadelphia to hash out once and for all the operating system of the United States of America. The fifty-five men ranged in age from their mid-twenties to eighty-one (Franklin). Washington was fifty-five. Madison was thirty-six. Hamilton was thirty. The average age was forty-two. Some were highly educated; some never went to college. Less than half were lawyers. Some believed in the Federalist agenda; some hated it. It was a loud, hot, boisterous, anxiety-ridden, nail-biter of a summer. Everyone in the country—and in the world because France, England, and Spain were watching closely, hoping for a way to rush in and take over—would have held their breath, but there was too much hot air in the air.

The debates, both during the Constitutional Convention and in every tavern, coffeehouse, and church social, were intense. The representatives were forced to compromise about almost everything, including slavery. Against the objections of Benjamin Franklin and others, slavery would be allowed to continue for another twenty years, gradually phasing out (although that would change). To satisfy the Southern states, each male slave would count as three-fifths of a citizen so that the slave-holding states would get more representatives in Congress. This became part of the Connecticut Compromise. It established a bicameral (two-room) legislature made up of a Senate, as per the New Jersey Plan, with two equal delegates from each state, and a House of Representatives, as per the Virginia Plan, with the number of representatives based on the population of each district within the states.

The final Constitution includes a Preamble that famously begins "We the People" in order to clarify the subject of the document. The whole text is 4,543 words long (including the signatures), making it the briefest as well as the oldest still-functioning Constitution in world history. (Most bills that go before Congress to be made into law are two or three times that length.)

The purpose of the Constitution is to limit the power of the federal government while at the same time giving the federal government the power to protect individual rights. The Founders believed in natural rights—the right to life, liberty, and the pursuit of happiness, as Jefferson put it in the Declaration. They also added the right to property, making sure that the possessions and businesses of individuals were protected from too much government interference.

The genius of the Constitution is that it's designed to be incomplete, a work in progress. The Founders wanted the document to be flexible enough to change with the times. They included a provision for the Constitution to be changed according to the will of the people through an amendment process. Madison's main intent was to protect individual rights, such as the right to a free press and the exercise of religion, the right to due process of law, and voting rights. These were provided for in an addendum, the Bill of Rights, that encouraged the Anti-Federalists to vote for it.

The Constitution was constitutionally ratified by nine states (the rest followed later) on June 21, 1788.

And the United States began again.

TAKEAWAY

The United States Constitution is a living document, changing and growing with the people it serves.

Customer Support

Invitation to recreate the United States

If you were a delegate to the Constitutional Convention in 1787, what would be your top three priorities to include in the new operating system?

1.

2.

3.

We the People

of the United [States]

ensure domestic Tranquility, provide for the common defence, promote the [general Welfare]
and our Posterity, do ordain and establish this Constitution for the [United States of America.]

Article. 1

Section. 1. All legislative Powers herein granted shall be vested in a Congress [of the United States,]
of Representatives.

Section. 2. The House of Representatives shall be composed of Members [chosen every second Year by the People of the several States,]
in each State shall have the Qualifications requisite for Electors of the most numerous B[ranch]

No Person shall be a Representative who shall not have attained to the [Age of]
and who shall not, when elected, be an Inhabitant of that State in which he shall [be chosen.]

Representatives and direct Taxes shall be apportioned among the several [States]
Numbers, which shall be determined by adding to the whole Number of free Persons,
not taxed, three fifths of all other Persons. The actual Enumeration shall [be made]
and within every subsequent Term of ten Years, in such Manner as they shall [by Law]
[thi]rty Thousand, but each State shall have at least one Representative; and [until such]
entitled to chuse three, Massachusetts eight, Rhode-Island and Providence [Plantations one,]
eight, Delaware one, Maryland six, Virginia ten, North Carolina five [South Carolina]

When vacancies happen in the Representation from any State, the [Executive]

The House of Representatives shall chuse their Speaker and other [Officers;]

Section. 3. The Senate of the United States shall be composed of two Senators [from each State]
Senator shall have one Vote.

Immediately after they shall be assembled in Consequence of the first [Election,]
of the Senators of the first Class shall be vacated at the Expiration of the [second Year,]
Class at the Expiration of the sixth Year, so that one third may be chosen every [second Year;]
Recess of the Legislature of any State, the Executive thereof may make temporary [Appointments]
such Vacancies.

No Person shall be a Senator who shall not have attained to the Age of [thirty Years,]
not, when elected, be an Inhabitant of that State for which he shall be chosen.

The Vice President of the United States shall be President of the Senate, but shall [have no Vote,]

The Senate shall chuse their other Officers, and also a President pro tempore, [in the Absence]
President of the United States.

The Senate shall have the sole Power to try all Impeachments. When sitting [for that Purpose,]
[when the President] of the United States, the Chief Justice shall preside: And no Person shall be convicted

Judgment in Cases of Impeachment shall not extend further than to removal

BASIC OPERATING INSTRUCTIONS

The following outline is an overview of how the Constitution came into being, how it works, its substance, and how it can change over time.

The Constitution: An Outline

I. ORIGINS

Articles of Confederation (1777, 1781 ratified)

1. "The United States must be a Firm League of Friendship."
   —John Dickinson (PA)
2. Government
   a. No unified court. Each state has independent courts.
   b. Unicameral Congress. Representatives from each state.
   c. No power to enforce laws between the states.
   (weak central government, semi-independent states)
   d. No power to raise taxes or pay for government or army.
3. Why popular?
   a. Allowed each state to rule itself.
4. Why it didn't work.
   a. Shays' Rebellion, 1786: MA taxes
      i. Tax rate higher than under British rule.
      ii. Land and property often confiscated.
      iii. Revolutionary War veterans felt cheated.

II. CONSTITUTIONAL CONVENTION, 1787

A. Federalism

1. Alexander Hamilton, James Madison, George Washington, John Adams
    a. Strong central government
        i. Can raise taxes to build infrastructure.
        ii. Checks and balances
            Government branches oversee one another.
        iii. Three co-equal branches of government
            Separation of powers
            1. Legislative – to create laws
            2. Executive – to enforce laws
            3. Judicial – to justify laws
    b. Industrial economy

Madison: *"If men were angels, government would not be necessary."*

B. Anti-Federalism

1. Thomas Jefferson, Patrick Henry, George Mason, Samuel Adams
    a. Strong state government
        i. Local government is best.
        ii. Each state chooses its government.
    b. Agricultural economy

Jefferson: *"The will of the majority is a sure guardian of the rights of man."*

C. How to Govern

1. New Jersey Plan—One state, one representative
2. Virginia Plan—Representatives by population
3. Connecticut Plan—Compromise
   Bicameral (two chambers) Congress
   a. Senate—Two senators, six-year term appointed by state legislatures (later changed to state-wide elections)
   b. House of Representatives—Elected by local districts, two-year terms

D. Three-Fifths Compromise

1. Northern states—Slaves didn't count for representation and taxes
2. Southern states—Feared Northern dominance if slaves didn't count
3. Compromise—Each male slave = 3/5 of a constituent
   (but they still couldn't vote)

III. PREAMBLE—MISSION STATEMENT

1. To **form a more perfect union** that continually improves
2. To **establish justice** with fair laws and open trials
3. To **insure domestic tranquility** and keep citizens safe
4. To **provide for the common defense** during war
5. To **promote the general welfare** fairly to everyone
6. To **insure the blessings of liberty** for the future

IV. STRUCTURE

A. Article One—Legislature (Congress—the Senate and the House of Representatives)

1. Makes laws
   - a. Both houses must approve by majority vote
   - b. President signs, or vetoes (objects)–
   - c. –Bill back to Congress, needs 2/3 majority
2. Approves treaties
3. Approves executive and judicial appointments
4. Funds armed forces
5. Declares war
6. Raises money (taxes)
7. Regulates commerce

B. Article Two—Executive (President)

1. President and vice president, four-year terms, elected by Electoral College delegates
2. Commander-in-chief of armed forces
3. Makes treaties and judicial appointments
4. Appoints cabinet (advisors)
5. Prepares budget
6. Conducts foreign policy

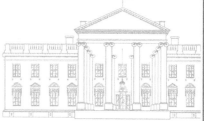

C. Article Three—Judiciary (Supreme Court)

1. Panel of justices, lifetime appointments
2. District and appellate courts, separate from states
3. Interprets the Constitution

D. Article Four—States have rights not in Constitution.

E. Article Five—Amendments require 2/3 of Congress, 3/4 of states.

F. Article Six—The Constitution is the absolute law of the land.

G. Article Seven—Ratification by 9 of the 13 of states.

V. THE BILL OF RIGHTS, 1791

1. Freedom of religion, speech, press, assembly, and petition
2. Freedom to own weapons for use in local militias
3. Soldiers not allowed to take over private houses
4. No unreasonable searches and seizures
5. No arrests without due process, no retrials, no self-incrimination
6. Speedy and public trials before a jury with a lawyer to assist defendants
7. Jury trial for civil and criminal cases
8. No unreasonable bail, no cruel and unusual punishment
9. Allows for more rights that may be listed later
10. Rights not granted to federal government go to states or individuals

FURTHER AMENDMENTS

There are an additional seventeen amendments to the Constitution:

11. Assures the authority of federal courts
12. Clarifies the election of the president and vice president
13-15. Gives former male (black) slaves the right to vote and further defines citizenship
16. Establishes a federal income tax
17. Changes the appointment of senators to state-wide popular elections
18, 21. Prohibits and then allows the consumption of alcohol
19. Gives adult women the vote
20. Clarifies terms of office for Congress and the president
22. Limits the president to two (four-year) terms
23. Allows D.C. residents a voice in presidential elections
24. Eliminates voting poll taxes
25. Clarifies presidential succession
26. Lowers the voting age to eighteen
27. Allows Congress to change salaries only after a new Congress takes office

YOUR CONSTITUTION

Because the Constitution is a constantly changing, living, and reactive document, the parts that no longer apply either through amendments, custom, or disuse have been printed in grey here.

The Preamble

Gouverneur Morris, an affable bon vivant and businessman from New York, who lost his leg in a carriage accident, gave the most speeches during the convention—mostly about how much the nation needed to protect religious tolerance and how little the nation needed slavery. Because of his flair for writing, Madison asked him to write the introduction to the Constitution, knowing it would be the most quoted part and that it had to be succinct and powerful. Morris's first three words capture the spirit of the Revolution and mark a true milestone in the history of humanity. He doesn't start with the expected "We the United States" or even "We the states." He goes right to the heart of the matter with "We the People." The word "People" was debated endlessly, but finally Madison convinced Washington that this nation and this Constitution is as much about the people, meaning you, reading this right now, as it is about the structures and regulations of the government. "We the People" set the tone for everything that followed.

Customer Support

THE PREAMBLE SCRAMBLE

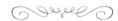

We the People of the United States, in Order to

1. form a more FUN RECEPTION,

2. establish ICE JUTS,

3. insure ACIDLY MOIST QUITRENT,

4. provide for CHEESED FOOTMMENN,

5. promote FREEWHEEL ANGER ART, and

6. RECUSE ENGLISH BEST BOYS TRIFLE

to ourselves and our Posterity, do ordain and establish this Constitution for the United States of America.

ARTICLE ONE: THE LEGISLATURE

Background: *The first article of the Constitution is the longest and the first for a reason. The Founders wanted three co-equal branches of government—the legislative, the executive, and the judicial—but they wanted the legislative branch to be a little more equal. Article One also contains the two big compromises of the Constitutional Convention. The first concerns how to count slaves—or as it's written, "other Persons." That doesn't sound great, but it's better than calling the African Americans in bondage "slaves." Some people think the Founders were tipping their hats to the future, hoping the next generation would do what they had failed to do—end slavery. Eighty years and the bloody Civil War later, that dream came true. The other great compromise was in how to structure the legislative branch. The delegates from New Jersey had a plan that called for every state to have one representative. Virginia's delegates realized that their state, the most populous at the time, would have the same number of votes as lowly Rhode Island. So they wanted each state to get representatives based on its population. This would give Virginia the most, of course. The delegates from Connecticut tried to save the states with smaller populations by coming up with a brilliant compromise. Congress would be bicameral, having two houses. The Senate would follow the New Jersey Plan, but with two senators from each state. The House of Representatives would follow the Virginia Plan with representatives based on the population. No one was happy and everyone was equally unhappy, and that is how Congress was born.*

Section 1. Congress

All legislative Powers herein granted shall be vested in a Congress of the United States, which shall consist of a Senate and House of Representatives.

Section 2. The House of Representatives

The House of Representatives shall be composed of Members chosen every second Year by the People of the several States

[The following refers to the individual states setting up their own requirements for who gets to vote.]

and the Electors in each State shall have the Qualifications requisite for Electors of the most numerous Branch of the State Legislature.

[Note: There were a lot of exceptions to "Electors," or voters, being exclusively white male property owners. For example, in New Jersey, women and African Americans were allowed to vote until 1807. Many of the newer western states gave women the vote decades before the Nineteenth Amendment gave all American women the vote in 1920.]

No Person shall be a Representative who shall not have attained to the Age of twenty five Years and been seven Years a Citizen of the United States, and who shall not, when elected, be an Inhabitant of that State in which he shall be chosen.

[The following is the Three-Fifths Compromise about counting three out of five slaves for taxing and for assigning representatives, later removed.]

Representatives and direct Taxes shall be apportioned among the several States which may be included within this Union, according to their respective Numbers, which shall be determined by adding to the whole Number of free Persons, including those bound to Service for a Term of Years, and excluding Indians not taxed, three fifths of all other Persons.

The actual Enumeration shall be made within three Years after the first Meeting of the Congress of the United States, and within every subsequent Term of ten Years, in such Manner as they shall by Law direct.

[Note the use of "persons" instead of "slaves," a subtle but important indication of things to come.]

The Number of Representatives shall not exceed one for every thirty Thousand, but each State shall have at Least one Representative;

[The following is the initial count of the first representatives from each state.]

and until such enumeration shall be made, the State of New Hampshire shall be entitled to choose three, Massachusetts eight, Rhode-Island and Providence Plantations one, Connecticut five, New-York six, New Jersey four, Pennsylvania eight, Delaware one, Maryland six, Virginia ten, North Carolina five, South Carolina five, and Georgia three.

[Today there are 435 members of Congress. The average population of the districts they represent is 710,767. The country has grown since 1789.]

When vacancies happen in the Representation from any State, the Executive Authority thereof shall issue Writs of Election to fill such vacancies.

The House of Representatives shall choose their Speaker and other Officers; and shall have the sole Power of Impeachment.

Customer Support

How often are members of the House of Representatives chosen?

What are the three requirements to be a member of the House?

1.

2.

3.

Section 3. The Senate

The Senate of the United States shall be composed of two Senators from each State

[The following was changed by the Seventeenth Amendment in 1913 when the election of senators was changed to a direct vote by the state population.]

chosen by the State Legislature thereof

for six Years; and each Senator shall have one Vote.

No Person shall be a Senator who shall not have attained to the Age of thirty Years and been nine Years a Citizen of the United States, and who shall not, when elected, be an Inhabitant of that State for which he shall be chosen.

The Vice President of the United States shall be President of the Senate, but shall have no Vote, unless they be equally divided.

The Senate shall choose their other Officers, and also a President pro tempore, in the Absence of the Vice President, or when he shall exercise the Office of President of the United States.

The Senate shall have the sole Power to try all Impeachments. When sitting for that purpose, they shall be on Oath or Affirmation. When the President of the United States is tried, the Chief Justice shall preside: And no Person shall be convicted without the Concurrence of two thirds of the Members present.

Judgment in Cases of Impeachment shall not extend further than to removal from Office, and disqualification to hold and enjoy any Office of honor, Trust or Profit under the United States: but the Party convicted shall nevertheless be liable and subject to Indictment, Trial, Judgment and Punishment, according to Law.

Customer Support

How many senators are there from each state?

How long do senators serve between elections?

What are the three requirements to be a senator?

1.

2.

3.

What is the role of the vice president in the Senate?

How many senators have to vote for impeachment for impeachment proceedings to begin?

Section 4. Election of Senators

The Times, Places and Manner of holding Elections for Senators and Representatives, shall be prescribed in each State by the Legislature thereof; but the Congress may at any time by Law make or alter such Regulations, except as to the Places of choosing Senators.

The Congress shall assemble at least once in every Year, and such Meeting shall be on the first Monday in December, unless they shall by Law appoint a different Day.

Customer Support

Who controls the election of senators?

Section 5. Rules of Procedure

Each House shall be the Judge of the Elections, Returns and Qualifications of its own Members, and a Majority of each shall constitute a Quorum to do Business; but a smaller Number may adjourn from day to day, and may be authorized to compel the Attendance of absent Members, in such Manner, and under such Penalties as each House may provide.

Each House may determine the Rules of its Proceedings, punish its Members for disorderly Behavior, and, with the Concurrence of two thirds, expel a Member.

Each House shall keep a Journal of its Proceedings, and from time to time publish the same, excepting such Parts as may in their Judgment require Secrecy; and the Yeas and Nays of the Members of either House on any question shall be entered on the Journal.

Neither House, during the Session of Congress, shall, without the Consent of the other, adjourn for more than three days, nor to any other Place than that in which the two Houses shall be sitting.

Customer Support

Why must each house of Congress keep a written record of its proceedings?

Section 6. Compensation

The Senators and Representatives shall receive a Compensation for their Services, to be ascertained by Law, and paid out of the Treasury of the United States. They shall in all Cases, except Treason, Felony and Breach of the Peace, be privileged from Arrest during their Attendance at the Session of their respective Houses, and in going to and returning from the same; and for any Speech or Debate in either House, they shall not be questioned in any other Place.

No Senator or Representative shall, during the Time for which he was elected, be appointed to any civil Office under the Authority of the United States; and no Person holding any Office under the United States, shall be a Member of either House during his Continuance in Office.

Customer Support

Research current salaries and pensions paid to members of Congress.

How much do senators get paid per year?

How much pension do they receive after they leave office?

How much do representatives get per year?

How much pension do they receive after they leave office?

Section 7. Voting

All Bills for raising Revenue shall originate in the House of Representatives; but the Senate may propose or concur as on other Bills.

Every Bill which shall have passed the House of Representatives and the Senate, shall, before it becomes a Law, be presented to the President of the United States; If he approves he shall sign it, but if not he shall return it with his Objections to that House in which it shall have originated to reconsider it.

If after such Reconsideration two thirds of that House shall agree to pass the Bill, it shall be sent, together with the Objections, to the other House, by which it shall likewise be reconsidered, and if approved by two thirds of that House, it shall become a Law. But in all such Cases the Votes of both Houses shall be determined by yeas and nays, and the Names of the Persons voting for and against the Bill shall be entered on the Journal of each House respectively.

[Yes, this may seem boring, but it's important. This is how laws are actually made.]

If any Bill shall not be returned by the President within ten Days (Sundays excepted) after it shall have been presented to him, the Same shall be a Law, in like Manner as if he had signed it, unless the Congress by their Adjournment prevent its Return, in which Case it shall not be a Law.

Every Order, Resolution, or Vote to which the Concurrence of the Senate and House of Representatives may be necessary (except on a question of Adjournment) shall be presented to the President of the United States; and before the Same shall take Effect, shall be approved by him, or being disapproved by him, shall be repassed by two thirds of the Senate and House of Representatives, according to the Rules and Limitations prescribed in the Case of a Bill.

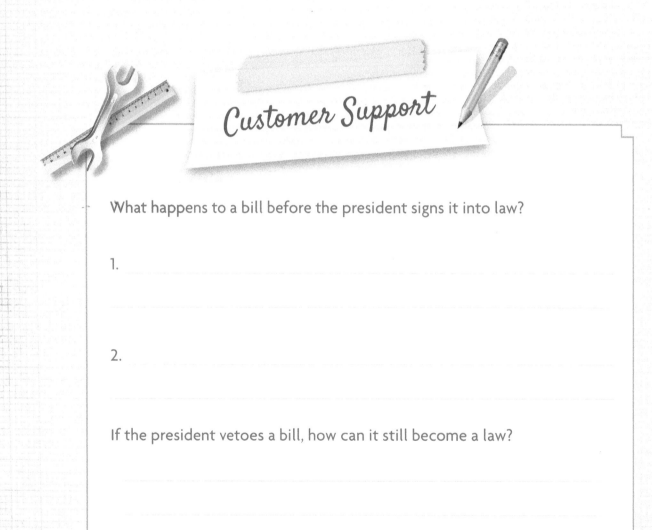

Customer Support

What happens to a bill before the president signs it into law?

1.

2.

If the president vetoes a bill, how can it still become a law?

Section 8. Powers

The Congress shall have Power

- To lay and collect Taxes, Duties, Imposts and Excises to pay the Debts and provide for the common Defense and general Welfare of the United States;

- To borrow Money on the credit of the United States;

- To regulate Commerce with foreign Nations, and among the several States, and with the Indian Tribes;

- To establish a uniform Rule of Naturalization,

- and uniform Laws on the subject of Bankruptcies throughout the United States;

- To coin Money, regulate the Value thereof, and of foreign Coin,

- and fix the Standard of Weights and Measures;

- To provide for the Punishment of counterfeiting the Securities and current Coin of the United States;

- To establish Post Offices and post Roads;

- To promote the Progress of Science and useful Arts, by securing for limited Times to Authors and Inventors the exclusive Right to their respective Writings and Discoveries;

- To constitute Tribunals inferior to the Supreme Court;

- To define and punish Piracies and Felonies committed on the high Seas, and Offences against the Law of Nations;

- To declare War,

- To grant Letters of Marque and Reprisal, and make Rules concerning Captures on Land and Water;

- To raise and support Armies, (but no Appropriation of Money to that Use shall be for a longer Term than two Years);

- To provide and maintain a Navy;

- To make Rules for the Government and Regulation of the land and naval Forces;

- To provide for calling forth the Militia to execute the Laws of the Union, suppress Insurrections and repel Invasions;

- To provide for organizing, arming, and disciplining, the Militia, and for governing such Part of them as may be employed in the Service of the United States, reserving to the States respectively, the Appointment of the Officers, and the Authority of training the Militia according to the discipline prescribed by Congress;

- To exercise exclusive Legislation in all Cases whatsoever, over such District (not exceeding ten Miles square) as may, by Cession of particular States, and the Acceptance of Congress, become the Seat of the Government of the United States, and to exercise like Authority over all Places purchased by the Consent of the Legislature of the State in which the Same shall be, for the Erection of Forts, Magazines, Arsenals, dock-Yards, and other needful Buildings;—And

- To make all Laws which shall be necessary and proper for carrying into Execution the foregoing Powers, and all other Powers vested by this Constitution in the Government of the United States, or in any Department or Officer thereof.

Customer Support

Research the answers to these questions.

1. Which wars has Congress actually declared?

2. Why does Congress control Washington, D.C.?

3. What laws has Congress passed under the "necessary and proper" clause?

Section 9. Powers Denied to Congress

- **The Migration or Importation of such Persons** *[Note: by "Persons," they mean slaves.]* **as any of the States now existing shall think proper to admit, shall not be prohibited by the Congress prior to the Year one thousand eight hundred and eight** *[1808]*, **but a Tax or duty may be imposed on such Importation, not exceeding ten dollars for each Person.**

- **The Privilege of the Writ of Habeas Corpus shall not be suspended, unless when in Cases of Rebellion or Invasion the public Safety may require it.**

- **No Bill of Attainder or ex post facto Law shall be passed.**

- **No capitation or direct Tax shall be laid, unless in Proportion to the Census or enumeration herein before directed to be taken.**

- **No Tax or Duty shall be laid on Articles exported from any State.**

- **No Preference shall be given by any Regulation of Commerce or Revenue to the Ports of one State over those of another: nor shall Vessels bound to, or from, one State, be obliged to enter, clear, or pay Duties in another.**

- **No Money shall be drawn from the Treasury, but in Consequence of Appropriations made by Law; and a regular Statement and Account of the Receipts and Expenditures of all public Money shall be published from time to time.**

- **No Title of Nobility shall be granted by the United States: And no Person holding any Office of Profit or Trust under them, shall, without the Consent of the Congress, accept of any present, Emolument, Office, or Title, of any kind whatever, from any King, Prince, or foreign State.**

Customer Support

Why did Congress want to stop the slave trade in 1808?

Research the following terms and define them.

Habeas corpus

Ex post facto

Section 10. Powers Denied to the States

- No State shall enter into any Treaty, Alliance, or Confederation; grant Letters of Marque and Reprisal; coin Money; emit Bills of Credit; make any Thing but gold and silver Coin a Tender in Payment of Debts; pass any Bill of Attainder, ex post facto Law, or Law impairing the Obligation of Contracts, or grant any Title of Nobility.

- No State shall, without the Consent of the Congress, lay any Imposts or Duties on Imports or Exports, except what may be absolutely necessary for executing its inspection Laws: and the net Produce of all Duties and Imposts, laid by any State on Imports or Exports, shall be for the Use of the Treasury of the United States; and all such Laws shall be subject to the Revision and Control of the Congress.

- No State shall, without the Consent of Congress, lay any Duty of Tonnage, keep Troops, or Ships of War in time of Peace, enter into any Agreement or Compact with another State, or with a foreign Power, or engage in War, unless actually invaded, or in such imminent Danger as will not admit of delay.

Customer Support

How does this section make the states more dependent on the federal, or central, government?

Comparison Between the House and Senate

	HOUSE OF REPRESENTATIVES	SENATE
Number of members		
How many per state?		
How long a term?		
Main responsibilities		

Customer Support

Defining Terms
Write the definitions of the following terms.

Quorum	
Session	
Term	
Census	
Amendment	
Liable	
Adjourn	
Treason	
Naturalization	
Bankrupt	
Patent	
Bill	
Veto	
Revenue	

TAKEAWAY

The United States Constitution is a living document, changing and growing with the people it serves.

ARTICLE TWO: THE EXECUTIVE

Background: *Despite how the media and popular entertainment might make it seem, the executive branch of government, specifically the office of the president, has very limited powers. This was very intentional on the part of the Founders. Their second biggest fear, after giving too much power to the people, was to concentrate too much power in one person's hands. They hated tyranny and kings, and went out of their way to make sure the American president would not become a despot. In the first election in February of 1789, George Washington became the first (and only) president to be unanimously elected. Already considered the "father" of his country and universally loved for his temperament, Washington was the right person for the job—though he didn't want it. "My movements to the chair of government," he wrote before the inauguration, "will be accompanied with feelings not unlike those of a culprit who is going to the place of his execution." The power of the president may wax and wane depending on the times and the personality, but the responsibility of the entire nation often rests on presidential shoulders. The executive branch is the largest branch of government with fifteen different departments headed by cabinet members and dozens of executive agencies (such as the Central Intelligence Agency) and commissions (such as the Federal Communications Commission). About two million people work in the executive branch. That's not counting the million and a half people in the military, who are under orders from the president. Though the powers are limited, they are there and the potential for misusing the office of the presidency is so great that the Founders put in firewalls, such as the impeachment process, to control it.*

Section 1. The Election of the President

The executive Power shall be vested in a President of the United States of America. He shall hold his Office during the Term of four Years, and, together with the Vice President, chosen for the same Term, be elected, as follows:

[The following describes the Electoral College. Electors, not the people, vote for the president. However, the Electors are chosen by the state governments (each state gets as many Electors as they have representatives), and, depending on the state, they are supposed to vote the will of the people. But they don't always. The Electoral College is designed so that states—not the people—vote for president.]

Each State shall appoint, in such Manner as the Legislature thereof may direct, a Number of Electors, equal to the whole Number of Senators and Representatives to which the State may be entitled in the Congress: but no Senator or Representative, or Person holding an Office of Trust or Profit under the United States, shall be appointed an Elector.

Customer Support

Research and give your opinion about the Electoral College.

The following was changed by the Twelfth Amendment in 1804 so that the vice president would be on the same political party ballot as the president and not, as here, the runner-up in presidential elections.]

The Electors shall meet in their respective States, and vote by Ballot for two Persons, of whom one at least shall not be an Inhabitant of the same State with themselves. And they shall make a List of all the Persons voted for, and of the Number of Votes for each; which List they shall sign and certify and transmit sealed to the Seat of the Government of the United States, directed to the President of the Senate. The President of the Senate shall, in the Presence of the Senate and House of Representatives, open all the Certificates, and the Votes shall then be counted. The Person having the greatest Number of Votes shall be the President, if such Number be a Majority of the whole Number of Electors appointed; and if there be more than one who have such Majority, and have an equal Number of Votes, then the House of Representatives shall immediately choose by Ballot one of them for President; and if no Person have a Majority, then from the five highest on the List the said House shall in like Manner choose the President. But in choosing the President, the Votes shall be taken by States, the Representation from each State having one Vote; A quorum for this Purpose shall consist of a Member or Members from two thirds of the States, and a Majority of all the States shall be necessary to a Choice. In every Case, after the Choice of the President, the Person having the greatest Number of Votes of the Electors shall be the Vice President. But if there should remain two or more who have equal Votes, the Senate shall choose from them by Ballot the Vice President.

The Congress may determine the Time of choosing the Electors, and the Day on which they shall give their Votes; which Day shall be the same throughout the United States.

No Person except a natural born Citizen, or a Citizen of the United States, at the time of the Adoption of this Constitution, shall be eligible to the Office of President; neither shall any person be eligible to that Office who shall not have attained to the Age of thirty five Years, and been fourteen Years a Resident within the United States.

[The following was changed by the Twenty-Fifth Amendment to clarify presidential succession.]

In Case of the Removal of the President from Office, or of his Death, Resignation, or Inability to discharge the Powers and Duties of the said Office, the Same shall devolve on the Vice-President, and the Congress may by Law provide for the Case of Removal, Death, Resignation or Inability, both of the President and Vice President, declaring what Officer shall then act as President, and such Officer shall act accordingly, until the Disability be removed, or a President shall be elected.

The President shall, at stated Times, receive for his Services, a Compensation, which shall neither be increased nor diminished during the Period for which he shall have been elected, and he shall not receive within that Period any other Emolument from the United States, or any of them.

[Note: The current salary for the U.S. president is $400,000 per year plus $50,000 for miscellaneous expenses, $100,000 for travel, and $19,000 for entertainment, plus free health care and a $200,000 per year pension for life. Of the forty-four people who served as president, only three refused the salary or gave it to charity: Herbert Hoover, John Kennedy, and Donald Trump.]

Before he enter on the Execution of his Office, he shall take the following Oath or Affirmation: "I do solemnly swear (or affirm) that I will faithfully execute the Office of President of the United States, and will to the best of my Ability, preserve, protect and defend the Constitution of the United States."

Customer Support

Who elects the president?

How long is the term for the president and vice president?

What are three qualifications to be elected president?

1.

2.

3.

Section 2. Presidential Powers

The President shall be Commander in Chief of the Army and Navy of the United States, and of the Militia of the several States, when called into the actual Service of the United States; he may require the Opinion, in writing, of the principal Officer in each of the executive Departments, upon any Subject relating to the Duties of their respective Offices, and he shall have Power to grant Reprieves and Pardons for Offenses against the United States, except in Cases of Impeachment.

He shall have Power, by and with the Advice and Consent of the Senate, to make Treaties, provided two thirds of the Senators present concur; and he shall nominate, and by and with the Advice and Consent of the Senate, shall appoint Ambassadors, other public Ministers and Consuls, Judges of the supreme Court, and all other Officers of the United States, whose Appointments are not herein otherwise provided for, and which shall be established by Law: but the Congress may by Law vest the Appointment of such inferior Officers, as they think proper, in the President alone, in the Courts of Law, or in the Heads of Departments.

The President shall have Power to fill up all Vacancies that may happen during the Recess of the Senate, by granting Commissions, which shall expire at the End of their next Session.

Customer Support

Your Opinion: Why did Congress limit the president's power to command the armed forces by the War Powers Resolution of 1973?

List three cabinet departments and their responsibilities.

Cabinet Department	Responsibilities

Section 3. State of the Union

He shall from time to time give to the Congress Information of the State of the Union, and recommend to their Consideration such Measures as he shall judge necessary and expedient; he may, on extraordinary Occasions, convene both Houses, or either of them, and in Case of Disagreement between them, with Respect to the Time of Adjournment, he may adjourn them to such Time as he shall think proper; he shall receive Ambassadors and other public Ministers; he shall take Care that the Laws be faithfully executed, and shall Commission all the Officers of the United States.

Customer Support

The "Take Care" clause allows for executive orders, a controversial use of power by the president that sidesteps Congress. Find an executive order and explain why you think it was good or bad for the country.

Executive Order:

Section 4. Impeachment

The President, Vice President and all civil Officers of the United States, shall be removed from Office on Impeachment for, and Conviction of, Treason, Bribery, or other high Crimes and Misdemeanors.

Customer Support

Research: Which presidents have been impeached?

President	Why Impeached	Results

PRESIDENTIAL CROSSWORD PUZZLE

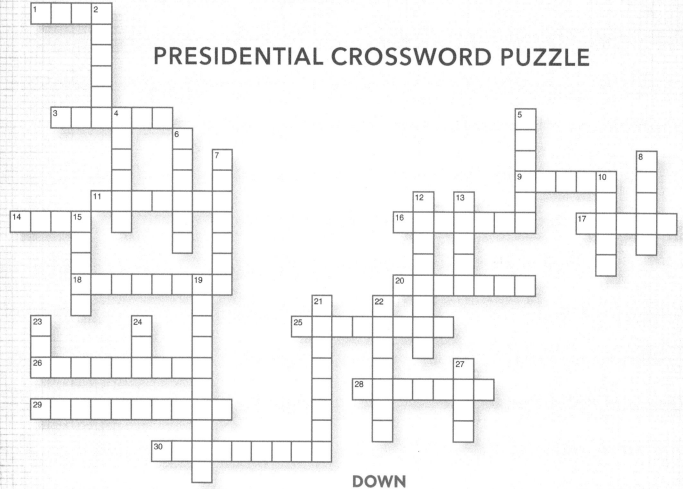

ACROSS

1. Worth one in the hand
3. Mr. Peanut
9. Won the Civil War
11. Bloody
14. The heaviest
16. Architect of the Constitution
17. Father and son
18. Third assassination witnessed by Lincoln's son
20. He's with Hillary
25. Grandfather and grandson
26. Monticello maestro
28. Impeached
29. Number one
30. Elected twice nonconsecutively

DOWN

2. Followed by FDR
4. Former hat salesman
5. Bonzo bedmate
6. Only one with a PhD
7. Camelot
8. Not born in Kenya
10. Bully for you
12. French version
13. Woebegone Watergater
15. No more an apprentice
19. Won World War II
21. Second assassination witnessed by Lincoln's son
22. The Great Emancipator
23. Vietnam quagmired
24. Four-term wonder
27. Not a car

TAKEAWAY

The president of the United States is elected to serve a four-year term. The president accepts or rejects all laws made by Congress (though Congress can override presidential vetoes) and, as leader of the executive branch, enforces those laws, appoints judges and ambassadors, and listens to the advice of cabinet members. The president is also the head of state and represents the nation with other nations, and is the commander-in-chief of the armed forces.

ARTICLE THREE: THE JUDICIARY

Background: *Alexander Hamilton once called it the weakest branch of government. Thomas Jefferson thought it overstepped its powers by establishing itself as the main interpreter of the Constitution. But the Supreme Court has become the keeper of the flame of the Constitution. Though the justices are appointed, not elected, they can decide that any law created by an elected Congress is invalid if found to be not consistent with the Constitution. It's probably the most influential part of the government. There is more to the judicial branch than the Supreme Court. The United States currently has thirteen appellate courts and ninety-four district courts. These are made up of judges appointed by the president and confirmed by Congress. About 10,000 cases every year make their way up the court system trying to get heard by the Supreme Court. SCOTUS (Supreme Court of the United States) accepts about one hundred of those cases to review. They usually pick cases that affect the entire nation and involve constitutional disputes such as, for example, a conflict between the First Amendment rights of free speech and free exercise of religious beliefs. The nine justices sit on a bench and hear lawyers make arguments that support or attack previous rulings by lower courts. Then they deliberate on each case independently and vote. Those justices who supported the winning side write majority opinions on the case. Those justices who voted against the majority often write dissenting opinions. The verdict of the Supreme Court establishes a legal precedent, or reference, for other cases in other courts. If the Supreme Court's decision contradicts a current law in the U.S. Congress or in state legislatures, that law has to be changed.*

Section 1. Judicial Structure

The judicial Power of the United States shall be vested in one supreme Court and in such inferior Courts as the Congress may from time to time ordain and establish. The Judges, both of the supreme and inferior Courts, shall hold their Offices during good Behavior and shall, at stated Times, receive for their Services a Compensation, which shall not be diminished during their Continuance in Office.

Customer Support

Why do Supreme Court justices have life terms ("good Behavior")?

Section 2. Judicial Powers

The judicial Power shall extend to all Cases, in Law and Equity, arising under this Constitution, the Laws of the United States, and Treaties made, or which shall be made, under their Authority; to all Cases affecting Ambassadors, other public Ministers and Consuls; to all Cases of admiralty and maritime Jurisdiction; to Controversies to which the United States shall be a Party; to Controversies between two or more States; between Citizens of different States; and between Citizens of the same State claiming Lands under Grants of different States.

In all Cases affecting Ambassadors, other public Ministers and Consuls, and those in which a State shall be Party, the supreme Court shall have original Jurisdiction. In all the other Cases before mentioned, the supreme Court shall have appellate Jurisdiction, both as to Law and Fact, with such Exceptions, and under such Regulations as the Congress shall make.

The Trial of all Crimes, except in Cases of Impeachment, shall be by Jury; and such Trial shall be held in the State where the said Crimes shall have been committed; but when not committed within any State, the Trial shall be at such Place or Places as the Congress may by Law have directed.

Customer Support

Research: Who are the current Supreme Court justices?

1.

2.

3.

4.

5.

6.

7.

8.

9.

Section 3. Treason

Treason against the United States shall consist only in levying War against them, or in adhering to their Enemies, giving them Aid and Comfort. No Person shall be convicted of Treason unless on the Testimony of two Witnesses to the same overt Act, or on Confession in open Court.

The Congress shall have Power to declare the Punishment of Treason, but no Attainder of Treason shall work Corruption of Blood, or Forfeiture except during the Life of the Person attainted.

Customer Support

Define "Corruption of Blood."

TAKEAWAY

The judicial branch determines whether a law is Constitutional. It consists of a Supreme Court with lifetime justices appointed by the president, as well as lower courts created by Congress. The Supreme Court is "the court of last resort" because its rulings are final.

ARTICLE FOUR: THE STATES

Background: *The first three articles cover the federal government and establish a system of checks and balances among the legislative, executive, and judicial branches. Article Four gives the Constitution an almost three-dimensional, ingenious approach to government by adding the layer of individual state governments. It ensures that each state will be a republic, a micro-version of the federal system, and that each state will respect the laws of all other states with "full faith and credit" so that a marriage in Delaware is still recognized in Alabama or a child in Alaska has the same rights as one in Florida (of course this is often an area of dispute, which gives the Supreme Court a lot to do—the worst example of states not interpreting laws the same way resulted in the Civil War). By and large, though, when you think about how different the states are, say California and Texas or Wisconsin and Mississippi, Article Four has held them all together, giving just enough local authority to be semi-independent from the national government, but also to keep the laws and customs somewhat consistent from state to state.*

Section 1. Respect Due to the States

Full Faith and Credit shall be given in each State to the public Acts, Records, and judicial Proceedings of every other State. And the Congress may by general Laws prescribe the Manner in which such Acts, Records and Proceedings shall be proved, and the Effect thereof.

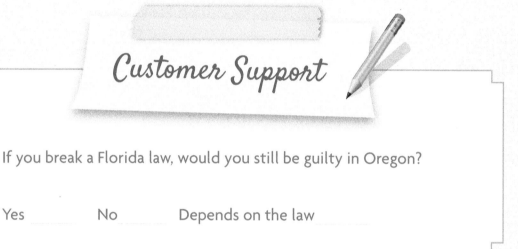

Customer Support

If you break a Florida law, would you still be guilty in Oregon?

Yes   No   Depends on the law

Section 2. Privileges Between States

The Citizens of each State shall be entitled to all Privileges and Immunities of Citizens in the several States.

A Person charged in any State with Treason, Felony, or other Crime, who shall flee from Justice, and be found in another State, shall on Demand of the executive Authority of the State from which he fled, be delivered up, to be removed to the State having Jurisdiction of the Crime.

[The following was cancelled out by the Thirteenth Amendment, which finally outlawed slavery.]

No Person held to Service or Labor in one State, under the Laws thereof, escaping into another, shall, in Consequence of any Law or Regulation therein, be discharged from such Service or Labor, but shall be delivered up on Claim of the Party to whom such Service or Labor may be due.

Customer Support

List the slave and free states as of 1789.

Slave states:

Free states:

Section 3. New States

New States may be admitted by the Congress into this Union; but no new State shall be formed or erected within the Jurisdiction of any other State; nor any State be formed by the Junction of two or more States, or Parts of States, without the Consent of the Legislatures of the States concerned as well as of the Congress.

The Congress shall have Power to dispose of and make all needful Rules and Regulations respecting the Territory or other Property belonging to the United States; and nothing in this Constitution shall be so construed as to Prejudice any Claims of the United States, or of any particular State.

Customer Support

Research why the following proposed states never made it.

Franklin:

Absaroka:

Transylvania:

Section 4. Guarantees

The United States shall guarantee to every State in this Union a Republican Form of Government and shall protect each of them against Invasion; and on Application of the Legislature, or of the Executive (when the Legislature cannot be convened) against domestic Violence.

Customer Support

Unscramble the key words in the following three definitions of a republican government.

1. Government gets its power from the **NERVEGOD**.

2. Those in power are **DECELET**.

3. **NATIVEPESTEERRS** govern according to law.

Article Four unites the states, making sure that they respect one another and the federal government.

ARTICLE FIVE: AMENDMENTS

Background: *It is not an exaggeration to say that without Article Five the Constitution would never exist. Article Five gives the Anti-Federalists what they most wanted, a way to change the government as necessary according to the changing times. The Founders were aware that the Constitution had to be a living document, that future generations would need to have a say in government. For many of them, this was how they addressed the problem of slavery—knowing that in a generation or two the majority would come around to realizing the evils of slavery. They envisioned other rights, as well, that would need protecting or defining, such as votes for women, marriage rights, labor laws, and issues regarding free speech and religion. Instead of having a bloody revolution every few years, as Jefferson thought, Madison built an ongoing revolution into the Constitution. It's not easy to make changes—or amendments—and only twenty-seven have been added, but even the understanding that the Constitution is not written in stone allows for, as Madison hoped, an ongoing conversation that never ends.*

Amendment Process

The Congress, whenever two thirds of both Houses shall deem it necessary, shall propose Amendments to this Constitution, or, on the Application of the Legislatures of two thirds of the several States, shall call a Convention for proposing Amendments, which, in either Case, shall be valid to all Intents and Purposes, as Part of this Constitution, when ratified by the Legislatures of three fourths of the several States, or by Conventions in three fourths thereof, as the one or the other Mode of Ratification may be proposed by the Congress;

[The following refers to banning of the slave trade, which the Founders thought inevitable, but to satisfy the Southern landowners they offered a twenty-year period before any formal ban could be put in place. It did become illegal to import slaves into the country after 1808 (though very loosely enforced). However, slavery continued until after the Civil War. During the war, Abraham Lincoln's Emancipation Proclamation freed slaves in the Southern states. The Thirteenth Amendment ended slavery all together in 1865 (though voting rights and civil right continued to be an issue for another hundred years). This passage became irrelevant after the Civil War.]

Provided that no Amendment which may be made prior to the Year One thousand eight hundred and eight shall in any Manner affect the first and fourth Clauses in the Ninth Section of the first Article;

[The following establishes that even states with different populations, say California and Wyoming, have the same representatives in the Senate (though in the House it's strictly by population) because the Senate is a place for states to debate their interests and the House is for the people to debate their interests.]

and that no State, without its Consent, shall be deprived of its equal Suffrage in the Senate.

What is needed for a new amendment to be added to the Constitution?

TAKEAWAY — *Article Five explains how the Constitution can be modified with amendments.*

ARTICLE SIX: CONSTITUTIONAL POWERS

Background: *Just to make everything perfectly clear, Article Six emphasizes that the Constitution is the supreme law of the land. No state constitution or local law or anything else, including religious laws, takes precedence over the Constitution. Article Six gave the Federalists what they most wanted, a clear hierarchy of government with the centralized power located in the Constitution. The Constitution can be changed through the amendment process or interpreted through the Supreme Court, but it is The Law. Everyone who works in federal, state, or local governments or in any level of the judicial system must swear an oath to uphold and defend—not the country or the government or the president—but the Constitution.*

Debts

All Debts contracted, and Engagements entered into, before the Adoption of this Constitution, shall be as valid against the United States under this Constitution, as under the Confederation.

Supreme Law

This Constitution, and the Laws of the United States which shall be made in Pursuance thereof; and all Treaties made, or which shall be made, under the Authority of the United States, shall be the supreme Law of the Land; and the Judges in every State shall be bound thereby, any Thing in the Constitution or Laws of any State to the Contrary notwithstanding.

Oaths

The Senators and Representatives before mentioned, and the Members of the several State Legislatures, and all executive and judicial Officers, both of the United States and of the several States, shall be bound by Oath or Affirmation, to support this Constitution; but no religious Test shall ever be required as a Qualification to any Office or public Trust under the United States.

TAKEAWAY

The Constitution is "the supreme law of the land."

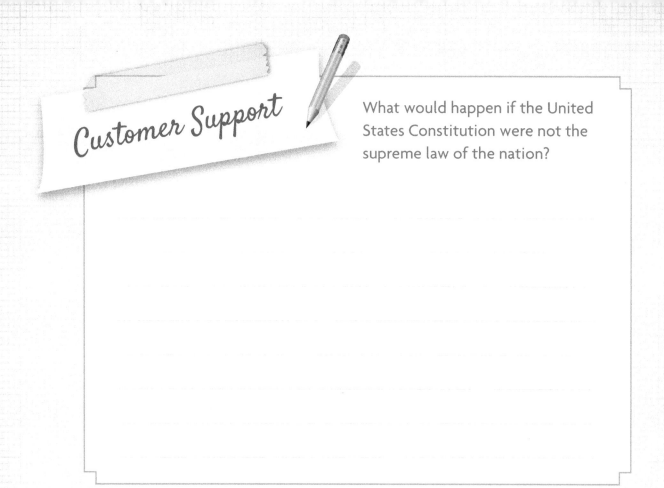

Customer Support

What would happen if the United States Constitution were not the supreme law of the nation?

ARTICLE SEVEN: RATIFICATION

Background: *The fatal flaw within the Constitution is that the whole thing is illegal. According to the Articles of the Confederation, which was still in effect, all the states had to agree on any change in government. The Constitution, by requiring only nine states to approve, violated the current law of the land. Even so, only thirty-nine of the fifty-five delegates signed the document at the time. The states each held conventions to decide on whether or not to vote for it. It took almost a year to get the required nine states, but four remained unconvinced. The two most populous states at the time, Virginia and New York, didn't sign until after it was approved. This is particularly ironic since Madison and Washington, who instigated the Constitutional Convention in the first place, were from Virginia, and Hamilton, who supported federalism, was from New York. Two states* *completely refused, though eventually North Carolina in 1789 and Rhode Island in 1790 did sign. The new, improved government of the United States began with the new Congress on March 4, 1789, in Federal Hall, New York City (the capital later moved to Congress Hall in Philadelphia in 1790 before settling in what would become Washington, D.C. in 1801).*

The Ratification of the Conventions of nine States, shall be sufficient for the Establishment of this Constitution between the States so ratifying the Same.

Customer Support

What do you think would have happened if fewer than nine states had ratified the Constitution?

TAKEAWAY

Article Seven makes the Constitution legal.

Sidebar: Slavery

The biggest problem for the nation at the time was slavery. What did the Founders really think of slavery? Almost all of them hated it. Even those that owned slaves, including Jefferson, Washington, and Madison, wanted it to end. Franklin (who briefly owned two slaves as a young man, an experience that caused him to become anti-slave and, as importantly, pro-equality), Hamilton, and Adams were active in early abolition movements. But in 1787, they needed to keep the Southern plantation owners in line. When the Southern states broke away from the Union over this issue, Abraham Lincoln led the Union into the Civil War. Finally, slavery ended in 1865 with the passage of the Thirteenth Amendment. Another century passed before the inalienable rights promised in the Declaration could be applied to more Americans through the Civil Rights Acts in the 1960s.

"There is not a man living who wishes more sincerely than I do to see a plan adopted for the abolition of slavery."
—George Washington

"To contend for our own liberty and to deny that blessing to others involves an inconsistency not to be excused."
—John Jay

"Every measure of prudence ought to be assumed for the eventual total extirpation of slavery from the United States. I hold the practice of slavery in abhorrence."
—John Adams

"Slavery is an atrocious debasement of human nature."
—Ben Franklin

"Slavery is fatal to religion and morality."
—Alexander Hamilton

"Nothing is more certainly written in the book of fate than that these people are to be free."
—Thomas Jefferson

"I believe a time will come when an opportunity will be offered to abolish this lamentable evil."
—Patrick Henry

"Slavery weakens the states; and such a trade is diabolical in itself and disgraceful to mankind."
—George Mason

"The inhabitant of Georgia and South Carolina who goes to the Coast of Africa and in defiance of the most sacred laws of humanity tears away his fellow creatures from their dearest connections and damns them to the most cruel bondage shall have more votes in a government instituted for protection of the rights of mankind than the Citizen of Pennsylvania or New Jersey who views with a laudable horror, so nefarious a practice."
—Gouverneur Morris

"We intend this Constitution to be the great charter of Human Liberty to the unborn millions who shall enjoy its protection, and who should never see that such an institution as slavery was ever known in our midst."
—James Madison

CUSTOMIZATION

One of the most brilliant ideas of the Founders was to add a process to change the Constitution within the Constitution. This makes the original contract with you, the user, subject to change. The entire United States is a permanent beta test with tons of modifications, add-ons, and plug-ins. Laws can be changed through the legislative process on the national, state, and local levels. But so can the structure of the government itself be tweaked, refined, purged, and updated through the amendment process. It's not easy, but it's been done many times. Here's how you can make your government work for you.

Summary of the Twenty-Seven Constitutional Amendments

The Constitution was ratified in 1788 with the understanding that a bill of rights would be attached immediately. The Anti-Federalists, who believed in the power of individuals over the state, wanted these amendments to guarantee that the power of the federal and state governments would be checked by these protections for individuals. The first ten amendments—the Bill of Rights—came in as a group in 1791, followed by the next two a few years later.

After the Civil War, the country and Congress finally started to repair the damage done by slavery and passed the Thirteenth, Fourteenth, and Fifteenth Amendments, which freed the slaves and gave former slaves full citizenship. In the decades since the Civil War, another twelve amendments were passed, covering a variety of issues as we'll see.

To add an amendment to the Constitution, two steps are required:

1. The proposed amendment must be voted in by two-thirds of the entire Congress (the House and the Senate)—or two-thirds of the state legislatures at a specially convened Constitutional Convention.
2. The approved amendment must then be ratified by three-fourths of the states.

THE BILL OF RIGHTS, 1791

The First Amendment

Congress shall make no law respecting an establishment of religion or prohibiting the free exercise thereof; or abridging the freedom of speech, or of the press; or the right of the people peaceably to assemble, and to petition the Government for a redress of grievances.

The forty-five words of the First Amendment are arguably the most important paragraph in American history, possibly even in the entire history of human beings living in social groups. It protects your essential forms of expression, your right to believe, think, say, share, and criticize pretty much anything. There are limits to that expression, as the Supreme Court will evaluate over the years—including whether you can yell "fire" when there isn't one in a crowded theater and whether the word "Congress" refers only to the national government and not to the states when it comes to making restrictive laws. But basically, the First Amendment guarantees that you have five freedoms:

1. Freedom of religion
2. Freedom of speech
3. Freedom of the press
4. Freedom of assembly
5. Freedom to complain

TAKEAWAY

The United States protects every individual's right to expression, thought, and belief (as long as that expression does not put others in danger).

Quick Question

How is hate speech protected by the First Amendment?

The Second Amendment

A well-regulated Militia, being necessary to the security of a free State, the right of the people to keep and bear Arms, shall not be infringed.

The Second Amendment is very controversial today. At the time, however, the United States had no standing army. The Revolutionary War was fought mostly by civilians with their own weapons. The Minutemen at Lexington and Concord were well-regulated militia. Today, however, we have a full military, including the National Guard, the modern version of Minutemen, as well as fully armed police forces. Many people, though, believe that individuals should be able, if they want, to own guns for personal protection, recreational use (target shooting and hunting), and as a means of defense against a possibly hostile government.

TAKEAWAY

Americans are allowed to own guns for their own protection against foreign and domestic enemies.

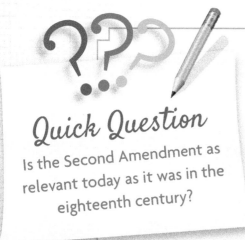

Quick Question

Is the Second Amendment as relevant today as it was in the eighteenth century?

The Third Amendment

No Soldier shall, in time of peace be quartered in any house, without the consent of the Owner, nor in time of war, but in a manner to be prescribed by law.

Arguably the most relevant to the people at the time, the Third Amendment prevents the government from using your private home to house soldiers without permission. During the Revolutionary War and before that, the British often commandeered homes for its men—displacing families from their own beds and costing them a fortune in feeding these men. It has also been cited as establishing "zones of privacy" for citizens as places where you don't have to worry about government interference.

TAKEAWAY

The government cannot just take away a person's home and possessions for its own use.

Quick Question

Why is the privacy of the home the foundation of a free society?

The Fourth Amendment

 **The right of the people to be secure in their persons, houses, papers, and effects, against unreasonable searches and seizures, shall not be violated, and no Warrants shall issue, but upon probable cause, supported by Oath or affirmation, and particularly describing the place to be searched, and the persons or things to be seized.**

Building on the Third Amendment, the Fourth Amendment goes even further in protecting your right, as Justice Louis Brandeis said, "to be left alone." The government cannot enter your house or arrest you or search you without a court order that includes "probable cause," a good reason for such action. What is "reasonable" in these cases depends on the times and the crimes. For example, airports are allowed to search passengers because of the risk of terrorism. Drivers can be routinely stopped because the consequences of driving while intoxicated are so great. But there is a lot of sensitivity about allowing the government to go too far, even in matters of personal or national security.

Note: there has been a lot of controversy about whether constitutional rights, especially the Fourth Amendment, applies to noncitizens either within the territorial United States or outside of it. For instance, does an undocumented immigrant have the same rights as a natural born citizen? Or does a native in another country have rights if, for example, he or she is being questioned by an American law enforcement agency? The short answer is yes, no, sometimes, and maybe. It really depends on the specific case. There have been more precedents lately for American constitutional rights to have more universal applications. Until the Supreme Court hears a case and weighs in, we'll have to wait for a more definitive answer.

TAKEAWAY

An individual's privacy cannot be violated without good cause, although there are many exceptions.

Quick Question

How much should the government be allowed to violate privacy to protect public safety?

The Fifth Amendment

No person shall be held to answer for a capital, or otherwise infamous crime, unless on a presentment or indictment of a Grand Jury, except in cases arising in the land or naval forces, or in the Militia, when in actual service in time of War or public danger; nor shall any person be subject for the same offence to be twice put in jeopardy of life or limb; nor shall be compelled in any criminal case to be a witness against himself, nor be deprived of life, liberty, or property, without due process of law; nor shall private property be taken for public use, without just compensation.

There's a lot to unpack within the Fifth Amendment. There are five rights that it guarantees you in case you get arrested (fingers crossed you don't—but in case):

1. It establishes that a grand jury can be called to decide whether a crime has been committed. Unlike regular court juries, the grand jury meets privately and secretly with the prosecutors and provides a check on the power of prosecutors.

2. The next protection is against "double jeopardy," which prevents the government from endlessly retrying cases where the defendant has already been found not guilty. It does not stop the government from retrying cases where there is new evidence or that have ended in a mistrial.

3. The famous "self-incrimination" clause protects you from testifying against yourself. An accused person can confess, but a confession cannot be forced through physical or psychological threats.

4. The fourth protection here is to make sure that you and all people accused of a crime are allowed the "due process of law," meaning that the law must be fair and that the trial must follow procedures such as the presumption of innocence and the stipulations laid out in the Sixth Amendment about trial by jury and having legal representation.

5. The final right in the Fifth Amendment is called "eminent domain." It means that the government cannot take your private property for its own use without compensating the property owner for the market value of the property. Note: The government can pay you to take your property if it needs to for the common good (building roads, preserving land, etc.).

TAKEAWAY

The government's power against individuals has very strong limitations.

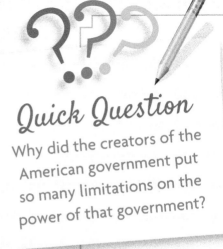

Quick Question

Why did the creators of the American government put so many limitations on the power of that government?

The Sixth Amendment

In all criminal prosecutions, the accused shall enjoy the right to a speedy and public trial, by an impartial jury of the State and district wherein the crime shall have been committed, which district shall have been previously ascertained by law, and to be informed of the nature and cause of the accusation; to be confronted with the witnesses against him; to have compulsory process for obtaining witnesses in his favor, and to have the Assistance of Counsel for his defense.

The Sixth Amendment also has many parts. All of them guarantee that certain procedures are followed in order that you get to have a fair trial. Among these are:

1. The right to have a trial as soon as possible.

2. Trials cannot happen in secret but must be open to the public and in or near the place where the crime happened.

3. Juries must be fair-minded and vetted by both prosecuting and defending lawyers (in a process known as *voir dire*—French for "to see and to say").

4. All charges must be made publicly.

5. The accused must have the right to directly confront all accusers.

6. All witnesses can be summoned to court via subpoenas (one must appear before court and would be "under penalty" if one doesn't). These seem obvious to us now, but historically this wasn't always the case.

7. Lastly, and perhaps most importantly, if you are ever accused of a crime, you must be able to have expert legal counsel to help you defend yourself in court and during interrogation by the police.

These rights form the heart and soul of the American legal system.

TAKEAWAY

The Sixth Amendment ensures that defendants have a chance to make a fair and rigorous argument against any charges against them.

Quick Question

If there are so many safeguards for the defendant, why would a defense attorney be necessary?

The Seventh Amendment

In suits at common law, where the value in controversy shall exceed twenty dollars, the right of trial by jury shall be preserved and no fact tried by a jury shall be otherwise re-examined in any Court of the United States than according to the rules of the common law.

Putting the twenty dollars aside (not relevant by today's value of money, but meant to indicate a substantial amount), the Seventh Amendment allows juries to decide both civil (nonfelonious disputes between private parties) and criminal cases. This means that often complex cases involving very specific information, such as patent rights to bioengineered pesticides or the manipulation of financial tools, would have to be decided by an empaneled jury of ordinary men and women, who are likely not experts in these fields. Some people have asked Congress to review this amendment on the grounds that expert juries are needed for complex cases, but the Supreme Court supports the amendment as written. The justices feel that it is up to the lawyers to make their cases using plain and compelling language. The second part of the amendment concerns the validity of a jury verdict. A judge cannot throw out a jury's verdict except if there was insufficient evidence for a guilty finding.

Quick Question

Can a civil trial involving complex and specific information be adequately evaluated by a nonspecialized, randomly selected jury?

TAKEAWAY

The Seventh Amendment guarantees that all legal cases, civil or criminal, can be heard by a jury and that a jury's decision cannot be dismissed by a judge.

The Eighth Amendment

Excessive bail shall not be required, nor excessive fines imposed, nor cruel and unusual punishments inflicted.

Bail is money or property offered to the court as a guarantee that you will appear in court and, until that court date, you can be set free. The Eighth Amendment restricts the court from setting the bail amount too high. It also protects you, if convicted, from paying fines that are too high or from getting punished in a manner out of proportion to the crime. For example, getting the death penalty for trespassing. The Eighth Amendment is often cited in cases involving torture, specifically of accused terrorists.

Quick Question

What justification could someone argue to defend torturing convicted terrorists?

TAKEAWAY

Even those accused and convicted of crimes have rights.

The Ninth Amendment

The enumeration in the Constitution of certain rights shall not be construed to deny or disparage others retained by the people.

In a way, the Ninth Amendment is the Bill of Rights of the Bill of Rights. Originally, the Bill of Rights was not included in the Constitution because the Founders wanted to emphasize that you have more rights than were included in the formal Constitution. They wanted an ongoing incentive for you to think about your rights and add them as necessary. The Ninth Amendment states that even this list of rights is not complete. There are more rights that you can have and that can be included in future amendments. What those rights are, who gets to have them, and how they appear as law are all matters for future generations, but they are still protected by the Constitution.

Quick Question

Who are the people that the Ninth Amendment claims can retain future rights? Are they individuals, states, judges, corporations, etc.?

TAKEAWAY

The Constitution continually insists that it be can changed by adding new rights for the people.

The Tenth Amendment

The powers not delegated to the United States by the Constitution, nor prohibited by it to the States, are reserved to the States respectively, or to the people.

Just as the Ninth Amendment promises future rights to the people, the Tenth Amendment promises that the individual states have powers that are not assigned to the federal government in the Constitution. It also says the people of those states have powers, as well. This was the key to the Anti-Federalist position, that you continue to have the power to control your life at the local level while the federal government functions in parallel. It assures that the United States actually consists of several governments with overlapping authority. This prevents power from becoming too centralized.

TAKEAWAY *The Constitution is determined to make sure power is distributed between federal and local governments.*

Quick Question
How could the interests of a state conflict with the interests of the entire nation?

BILL OF RIGHTS MATCH-UP

Connect the content of the amendment to its number.

1

2

3

4

5

BEAR ARMS

SPEEDY TRIAL

SEARCHES & SEIZURES

POWERS TO THE STATES

QUARTERING TROOPS

POWERS TO THE PEOPLE

BAIL & PUNISHMENT

CIVIL SUITS

RIGHTS OF THE ACCUSED

FREEDOM OF EXPRESSION

6

7

8

9

10

Answers on Page 160

ADDITIONAL AMENDMENTS

The Housekeeping Amendments: 11th, 16th, 25th & 27th

These amendments clarify certain powers and procedures of the federal government.

The Eleventh Amendment (1795)

Sovereign Immunity

Under a legal term known as "sovereign immunity," you can't sue your state or any other state unless a federal court grants special permission.

TAKEAWAY

The Sixteenth Amendment (1913)

Income Tax

TAKEAWAY

Everyone's least favorite amendment led to the government being allowed to collect a federal income tax from you in order to pay for the military, the federal bureaucracy, and social programs.

The Twenty-Fifth Amendment (1967)

Presidential Vacancy

If the president dies or can't do the job, the vice president takes over. If the vice president and a majority of the cabinet members think the president can't do the job, the speaker of the house and the president pro tempore (leading member) of the Senate can appoint the vice president to take over (the president can also contest that decision).

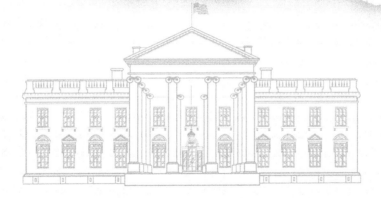

The Twenty-Seventh Amendment (1992)

Congressional Salaries

The current Congress cannot give itself a pay raise. It can vote on a pay raise only for the next Congress elected.

The Citizenship Amendments:
13th, 14th, 15th, 19th, 23rd, 24th & 26th

These amendments finish the work started with the Declaration in 1776. The Thirteenth, Fourteenth, and Fifteenth Amendments restore African American males to full citizenship after centuries of slavery and the bloody Civil War. Women, however, still had to wait until 1920 to be considered citizens in full.

The Thirteenth Amendment (1865)

Abolishes Slavery

TAKEAWAY

The jewel of Lincoln's legacy, the Thirteenth Amendment ends the "peculiar institution" of slavery. Racism, however, endured.

SHALL FREEDOM OR SLAVERY TRIUMPH. LET MASSACHUSETTS SPEAK!

The Fourteenth Amendment (1868)

Redefines Citizenship

Ending slavery wasn't enough. The Fourteenth Amendment ensures that African Americans have full citizenship and can vote (males only still). There are three basic ideas in this amendment:

1. Everyone born in the U.S.A. is an American citizen.
2. Once someone is a citizen by birth or by naturalization, that citizenship can never be taken away (except in extraordinary circumstances or voluntarily).
3. All citizens have "equal protection of the laws."

This amendment tried (and did not quite succeed) in eliminating discrimination.

The Fifteenth Amendment (1870)

Voting Rights for All Men

Technically, this amendment gives all men—particularly men who had been slaves—the right to vote. However, African Americans continued to be denied the vote in many places across the nation until Congress passed the Civil Rights Acts a hundred years after the Civil War.

The Nineteenth Amendment (1920)

Voting Rights for Women

Women had been struggling to get the vote—and therefore full citizenship—since the Revolution. Finally, this amendment gives women the right to vote and prohibits sexual discrimination at the voting polls.

The Twenty-Third Amendment (1961)

D.C. Voting

Somehow, residents of Washington, D.C., were left without representation in Congress or the right to vote for president. This amendment allows them three Electors in presidential elections. They still have no representation in Congress.

The Twenty-Fourth Amendment (1964)

Prohibits Poll Taxes

Poll taxes were charged to people who wanted to vote. It was prohibitory to poor people and to those often discriminated against—and used to keep them from voting. This amendment ended that.

The Twenty-Sixth Amendment (1971)

Lowers Voting Age

This amendment lowers the voting age to eighteen—particularly important during this time when eighteen-year-olds were being drafted into the Vietnam War.

The Prohibition Amendments: 18th & 21st

These are a good example of how governments, like people, can change their minds.

The Eighteenth Amendment (1919)

Prohibits Alcohol

The Temperance Movement of the late nineteenth century made the government think if it banned alcohol, it could reduce crime and improve lives.

The Twenty-First Amendment (1933)

Repeals Prohibition

The government was wrong. Prohibition made crime go up with illegal alcohol sales and reduced the quality of life considerably.

The Terms of Office Amendments: 12th, 17th, 20th & 22nd

The following refine some of the details about elections and office terms.

The Twelfth Amendment (1804)

Refined the Electoral College

You don't vote for president. Your Electors vote for president. This amendment now made the number of Electors for each state the number of their Representatives plus their two Senators. After Election Day, they cast their votes—theoretically but not always necessarily—reflecting the votes of the people. If there's a tie, the House votes for president and the Senate for vice-president.

The Seventeenth Amendment (1913)

Senatorial Elections

This amendment changes Article I of the Constitution. Instead of senators getting appointed by state legislatures, they now can be elected directly by a popular vote. The governor of your state can temporarily appoint someone to fill a vacant senate seat.

The Twentieth Amendment (1933)

Start of Term

The Twentieth Amendment moved the start of terms for elected federal officials from March to January to cut down on the "lame duck" period after the November elections when the previous officeholders had little power but could make things difficult for the new occupants. This amendment also cleared up presidential succession. If the president dies, the vice president takes over, then the speaker of the house, then the president pro tempore of the Senate, then the secretary of state, then (according to a 1947 law) the secretary of the treasury, the secretary of defense, the attorney general, and so on through the cabinet.

The Twenty-Second Amendment (1951)

Presidential Term Limits

This amendment limits the president to a maximum of two four-year terms or a maximum of ten years (if, for example, he or she takes over for a previous president).

Customer Support

Which amendment would best answer the following problems?

1. Mrs. Pye wishes she could change things in Congress.

2. Mr. Kew is happy to get a drink.

3. Ms. Lol had to graduate high school before voting.

4. Senator Shoo never ran for office in his life.

5. Mr. Tell thought he couldn't vote because he was an ex-slave.

6. Mrs. Tell didn't think they could afford to vote.

7. Ms. Woll doesn't get why the most popular candidate lost.

8. Ms. Bis couldn't wait four months to become president.

9. Mrs. Kew is glad Mr. Kew can no longer drink.

10. Mr. Tell knew he had the same rights as Mr. Kew.

11. President Bis feared Vice President Shoo wanted her job.

12. Mr. Pug tried to sue Mississippi, but he could only spell it.

13. Mr. and Mrs. Tell were so happy not to be slaves.

14. Dr. Gush called April 15 the day of national robbery.

15. President Bis wished she could run for a third term.

16. Senator Shoo voted for his opponent to get a raise.

17. Mr. and Mrs. Tell moved to D.C. and lost their vote.

Possible Future Amendments

1. **Equal Rights:** To guarantee equal legal rights to men and women in terms of employment, property ownership, etc. First introduced in 1921.

2. **Balanced Budget:** To prevent the federal government from spending more money than it takes in from taxes, etc.

3. **Term Limits:** To limit the time in office among congressional members and Supreme Court justices.

4. **Campaign Finance:** To limit the amount of money presidential and congressional candidates can take.

5. **Ending the Electoral College:** To provide for the direct election of president.

The Second Bill of Rights

Franklin Delano Roosevelt led the nation through its worst economic crises during the Great Depression in the 1930s, and the most large-scale war in its history, World War II, in the 1940s. During his State of the Union speech in 1944, hailed as one of the most important in history, Roosevelt laid out a plan for eight additional amendments that would be bundled together as essential rights for every American citizen. His plan never passed through Congress.

Many nations around the world in the post-war environment of national independence adopted many or all of FDR's ideas, including Iraq, Finland, Norway, Spain, Brazil, Ukraine, South Africa, Peru, Egypt, India, and even Russia. FDR's ideas became the centerpiece of the Universal Declaration of Human Rights by the United Nations. Slowly, they are beginning to be promoted in the United States, as well.

Here they are:

1. The right to a useful and remunerative job in the industries or shops or farms or mines of the nation;

2. The right to earn enough to provide adequate food and clothing and recreation;

3. The right of every farmer to raise and sell his products at a return which will give him and his family a decent living;

4. The right of every businessman, large and small, to trade in an atmosphere of freedom from unfair competition and domination by monopolies at home or abroad;

5. The right of every family to a decent home;

6. The right to adequate medical care and the opportunity to achieve and enjoy good health;

7. The right to adequate protection from the economic fears of old age, sickness, accident, and unemployment;

8. The right to a good education.

Customer Support

Why would you vote or not vote to ratify the possible future amendments or the second bill of rights? Which ones would be most important to you?

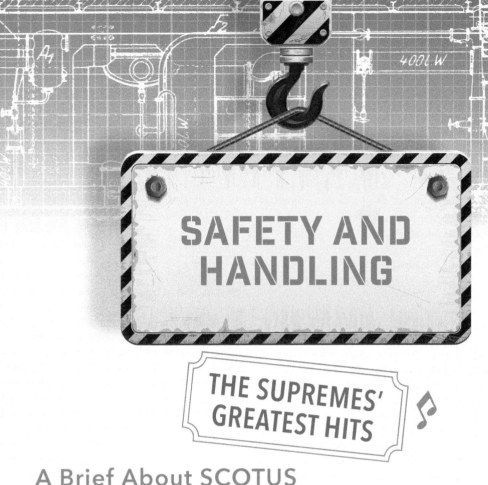

SAFETY AND HANDLING

THE SUPREMES' GREATEST HITS

A Brief About SCOTUS
The Supreme Court of the United States

The federal court system under Article III of the Constitution consists of:

- The Supreme Court,

- Thirteen circuit courts (for appeals or retrials),

- Ninety-four district courts (for trials), and

- Several lower courts.

All of the federal courts work separately from the individual state courts. In some cases, a criminal or civil case can be brought before either a federal or a state court. This depends on the legal strategy of the defendant and the plaintiff (one who complains against a defendant).

The Supreme Court

- Currently has nine justices (one is the chief justice), but the number of justices has varied over history from six to ten. In 1948, federal law set the number at nine.

- Cases go to the Supreme Court only if the Supreme Court decides there is a constitutional issue or a federal law in the case that needs to be reconsidered.

- The Supreme Court meets on the first Monday in October of each year and ends in early summer.

- Out of 7,000 annual petitions, they hear about 100 cases that they review and decide about by the end of the term. They listen to arguments presented by attorneys and read previous decisions. Each justice considers the merits of the case privately and in conference before they write their opinion. The presiding opinion is decided by majority vote.

- The Supreme Court justices, as all federal judges, are appointed by the president, approved by the Senate, and serve life terms.

Nine Landmark Supreme Court Cases

1. Marbury v. Madison (1803)

Impact: This decision established that only the judicial branch can determine whether a law is consistent with the Constitution, and that the Supreme Court is the only authority than can declare a law unconstitutional.

Background: Before leaving office, President John Adams appointed William Marbury to be a federal judge, along with several others. But when the new president, Thomas Jefferson, took office, he ordered his secretary of state, James Madison, to withdraw the appointments. Marbury petitioned the Supreme Court to force the government to honor the appointments.

Result: The Court decided 4–0 that Marbury and the others were right. The government had denied them their properly attained appointments. But the Court also ruled that it could not force the government to fulfill those promises. On one hand, Chief Justice John Marshall gave Jefferson what he wanted, but at the same time he established that the Supreme Court had the right to review and decide on the law. The ruling gave the Supreme Court more power than Jefferson wanted. Marshall's ruling introduced the concept of judicial review, that laws can be evaluated by the Court to make sure they are consistent with the Constitution. "It is emphatically the province and duty of the judicial department to say what the law is," wrote Marshall in his opinion. "An act of the legislature repugnant to the constitution is void." Not only did he out-maneuver Jefferson with this ruling, but Marshall also gave Madison a lesson on the Constitution that he had designed.

You Judge

Research this case and form your own opinion.

Guiding Question

Why should the Court, with its lifetime appointees, have final say about the Constitution?

2. Dred Scott v. Sandford (1857)

Impact: A devastating blow to African Americans, the court refused to acknowledge the potential citizenship of former slaves.

Background: Born a slave in Virginia, Dred Scott was sold to an army surgeon who moved to Wisconsin, a free territory, in 1836. While technically free, Scott married (which slaves could not do). Two years later, Scott and his wife had a daughter, technically born free in the free state of Illinois. After the surgeon died in 1843, his widow Irene claimed that she owned Scott, his wife, and their child, and had the right to rent him out in Iowa, also a free territory. After she died, her brother, John Sandford, sued to keep possession of Scott and his family.

Result: In a 7–2 decision, the Court overruled a lower court that had given Scott his freedom. Chief Justice Roger Taney wrote, "The question is simply this: Can a negro, whose ancestors were imported into this country, and sold as slaves, become a member of the political community formed and brought into existence by the Constitution of the United States, and as such become entitled to all of the rights, and privileges, and immunities, guaranteed by that instrument to the citizen?" The answer, according to the Supreme Court at the time, was no. And that answer led directly to the Civil War.

You Judge

Research this case and form your own opinion.

Guiding Question

How can someone be a slave where slavery is against the law?

3. Plessy v. Ferguson (1896)

Impact: This decision continued the segregation of black people and white people and made separating the "races" legal in schools, hospitals, and other institutions as long as the facilities were of equal quality.

Background: After the Civil War in 1865, the federal government provided protection for the newly freed slaves. But when federal troops were withdrawn from the South, the Southern states passed "Jim Crow" laws prohibiting black people from using the same services as white people. In 1892, Homer Plessy, a black man, boarded a whites-only railroad car and was arrested.

Result: The separate but equal doctrine promoted continued racial prejudice and established racist policies in federal and local institutions. The Court voted 7–1 against Plessy and ushered in an era of severe racial segregation that eventually prompted the Civil Rights movement in the 1950s. "The argument," wrote Justice Henry Billings Brown, "assumes that social prejudice may be overcome by legislation and that equal rights cannot be secured except by an enforced commingling of the two races."

You Judge

Research this case and form your own opinion.

Guiding Question

How can there be equality if there is forced separation?

4. Schenck v. U.S. (1919)

Impact: The freedom of speech protection clause in the First Amendment to the Constitution does not protect the speaker or the writer if what's spoken or written represents a "clear and present danger" to society.

Background: At the outbreak of American involvement in World War I, Charles Schenk, the general secretary of the American Socialist Party, printed pamphlets urging young men to resist the draft. This was a clear violation of the Espionage Act of 1917, which made it illegal during wartime for anyone to "interfere with the operation of the military forces of the United States." Schenk argued that the act itself was unconstitutional and a violation of the First Amendment.

Result: The Court decided unanimously against Schenk. The law referred to any operation that succeeded against the U.S. military, but encouraging people to not join was considered to be dangerous to military operations. As for the freedom of speech clause, Justice Oliver Wendell Holmes Jr. wrote, in one of the Court's most famous opinions, that "the most stringent protection of free speech would not protect a man in falsely shouting fire in a theatre and causing a panic. The question in every case is whether the words used are used in such circumstances and are of such a nature as to create a clear and present danger that they will bring about the substantive evils that Congress has a right to prevent."

You Judge

Research this case and form your own opinion.

Guiding Question

Under what circumstances does national security take precedence over freedom of speech?

5. Brown v. Board of Education (1954)

Impact: This decision reversed *Plessy v. Ferguson* and allowed for the integration of public institutions.

Background: Oliver Brown was a church deacon whose daughter, a third grader, had to take a long bus ride to get to her black school, while a white school was only a few blocks from her home. Brown sued the school board of Topeka, Kansas, to allow his daughter to attend the more local school.

Result: When Chief Justice Earl Warren wrote that "separate is inherently unequal," he spearheaded the Civil Rights Movements of the 1950s and 1960s. By a unanimous 9–0 decision, the Court ruled that the ruling in *Plessy v. Ferguson* was, in fact, unconstitutional. It upheld that equal rights were given all citizens under the Fourteenth Amendment. Warren continued, "Segregation of children in public schools solely on the basis of race deprives children of the minority group equal educational opportunities, even though the physical facilities and other 'tangible' factors may be equal. The 'separate but equal' doctrine adopted in *Plessy v. Ferguson* has no place in the field of public education." All schools across the United States were ordered to integrate. When a school district refused, as happened in Alabama, the National Guard was sent in to ensure that black and white children could attend school together.

You Judge

Research this case and form your own opinion.

Guiding Question

Why did it take so long for the Court to recognize the promise of equality offered in the Constitution?

6. Engel v. Vitale (1962)

Impact: The court banned prayer in public school in a 6–1 decision that reinforced the separation of church and state.

Background: The New York State Board of Regents, which controlled the school system, encouraged classes to begin with a prayer in addition to the Pledge of Allegiance (which already references "God"). Several families in New Hyde Park led by Steven Engel sued the local school board led by William Vitale. The plaintiffs were not atheists but claimed that any prayer conflicts with the establishment clause in the First Amendment ("Congress shall make no law respecting an establishment of religion") with a prayer addressed to "Almighty God."

Result: This decision did not outlaw prayer in school but limited a school's ability to force students to pray. It is one of many cases that seek to clarify what constitutes prayer in school and it is often used as a precedent to support other arguments. For the majority, Justice Hugo Black wrote, "It is no part of the business of government to compose official prayers for any group of the American people to recite as a part of a religious program carried on by government."

You Judge

Research this case and form your own opinion.

Guiding Question

What place does religion or spirituality have in public schools?

7. Miranda v. Arizona (1966)

Impact: The ruling requires that all law enforcement officers inform people they arrest that they have constitutional rights. The mandatory explanation of these rights are as follows: *"You have the right to remain silent. Anything you say can and will be used against you in a court of law. You have the right to an attorney. If you cannot afford an attorney, one will be provided for you. Do you understand the rights I have just read to you? With these rights in mind, do you wish to speak to me?*

Background: In 1963, Ernesto Miranda was arrested in Phoenix, Arizona, and charged with several felonies. With limited education, a history of mental instability, and no lawyer present, Miranda was interrogated for several hours and then plead guilty. Miranda then accused the police of not informing him of his Fifth and Sixth Amendment rights against self-incrimination and having access to legal counsel.

Result: In a controversial 5–4 decision, the Court found in favor of Miranda. His confession was ruled as inadmissible as evidence because the police failed to inform him of his rights. Chief Justice Earl Warren wrote that the Fifth Amendment is "fundamental to our system of constitutional rule" and necessary because a defendant "is not in the presence of persons acting solely in his interests." As a sidenote, Miranda was later retried with new evidence and after being read his rights. He was found guilty.

You Judge

Research this case and form your own opinion.

Guiding Question

Why should police be so concerned with the rights of alleged criminals?

8. Roe v. Wade (1973)

Impact: This 7–2 decision by the Court required forty-six states to change their laws regarding abortion and the rights of privacy. It allowed that a woman has a right to control her body, including her pregnancy during the first trimester. Individual and state authority over the pregnancy during the second and third trimesters would vary among the different states.

Background: In 1969, "Jane Roe" (an alias) became pregnant with her third child and was prevented from having an abortion by Texas state law. She had the baby and later sued Dallas District Attorney Henry Wade. The case went to the Supreme Court and was decided in Roe's favor in 1973. The constitutional issue was not about abortion, which is not mentioned in the Constitution, as the dissenting justices asserted, but about the Ninth and Fourteenth Amendments. The Ninth Amendment establishes that any rights not mentioned in the Constitution are reserved for individuals. These rights were purposely not included because the Founders wanted there to be some agency for individuals to have rights not regulated by the federal or state governments. In this case, it is used to support a woman's right to control her body. The Fourteenth Amendment protects "due process," asserting that not allowing a woman to have an abortion exerts an illegal control over her body by the state. However, the Fourteenth Amendment is often used by the dissenters of *Roe v. Wade* to argue for the due process rights of the unborn fetus, which they argue is also a person.

Result: *Roe v. Wade* allowed for women to have a choice about their pregnancy in the first trimester. Controversy continues because states and local groups disagree about whether abortion can take place beyond the first trimester, or if the termination of a pregnancy at any time deprives an unborn person of the fundamental right to life. Interestingly, the original litigant, Jane Roe, whose real name was Norma McCorvey, sued to have the decision reversed and became an anti-abortion activist during the last years of her life. This debate continues with strong feelings on both sides.

You Judge

Research this case and form your own opinion.

Guiding Question
How can the Court decide what a person is?

9. Citizens United v. Federal Election Commission (2010)

Impact: According to SCOTUS, corporations are covered under the First Amendment guarantee of free speech. It means that the government cannot stop a corporation or a union from spending money (a form of free speech or expression) to support or to attack any political candidate it chooses.

Background: During the presidential campaign of 2008, a conservative group, Citizens United, produced and distributed a film critical of then-candidate Hillary Clinton. The Federal Election Commission (FEC) had a law in place to prevent companies from paying for political statements, as Citizens United was about to do by buying time on cable TV stations to air their film. Citizens United then sought an injunction to prevent the FEC from suing them. After lower courts denied the injunction, the case went to the Supreme Court.

Result: In a very contentious 5–4 decision, the Court found in favor of Citizens United. Justice Anthony Kennedy wrote that the freedom of speech included "the freedom to speak in association with other individuals, including association in the corporate form." In a scathing dissent, Justice John Paul Stevens wrote, "The Court's blinkered and aphoristic approach to the First Amendment will undoubtedly cripple the ability of ordinary citizens, Congress, and the States to adopt even limited measures to protect against corporate domination of the electoral process. Americans may be forgiven if they do not feel the Court has advanced the cause of self-government today."

You Judge

Research this case and form your own opinion.

Guiding Question

How can corporations be considered to have the same rights as individuals?

SUPPORT AND FAQS

Answer some of these questions in essay form. Explain your opinion based on your understanding of the Constitution, the amendments, Supreme Court decisions, and history.

What do you think of the American political system?

What do you think of political parties?

How do you understand the concept of term limits?

How would you control money in campaigns?

$ $ $

What is your opinion of opinion polls?

Under what circumstances would you support the death penalty?
If you don't support it, why not?

Why should there be more or fewer gun regulations?

How should the media be controlled, if at all?

How does religion work, if at all, in government?

Why are income taxes constitutional?

When, if ever, should constitutional rights be suspended?

When, if ever, would security be more important than freedom?

Should the United States police the world?

Should the United States spread democracy?

Should there be reparations for slavery?

Should there be reparations for taking Native American lands?

What citizens' rights did the Founders leave out?

Who qualifies to be an American citizen?

How does the American Revolution continue?

CLOSING

"When the architects of our republic wrote the magnificent words of the Constitution and the Declaration of Independence, they were signing a promissory note to which every American was to fall heir. This note was a promise that all men, yes black men as well as white men, would be guaranteed the inalienable rights of life, liberty, and the pursuit of happiness."—Martin Luther King Jr.

"The strength of the Constitution lies entirely in the determination of each citizen to defend it. Only if every single citizen feels duty bound to do his share in this defense are the constitutional rights secure."
—Albert Einstein

"Every Constitution written since the end of World War II includes a provision that men and women are citizens of equal stature. Ours does not."—Ruth Bader Ginsburg

"Constitutional democracy, you see, is no romantic notion. It's our defense against ourselves, the one foe who might defeat us."
—Bill Moyers

"If the Constitution was a movie, the Preamble would be the trailer, the First Amendment the establishing shot, the 13th the crowd pleaser and the 14th the ultimate hero scene."—Henry Rollins

The Constitution of the United States of America is yours. Use it or lose it.

Page 37 Answers:

1-F, 2-AF, 3-AF, 4-F, 5-AF, 6-F

Page 117 Answers:

1-freedoms of expression, 2-bear arms, 3-quartering troops, 4-searches and seizures, 5-rights of accused, 6-speedy trial, 7-civil suits, 8-bail and punishment, 9-powers to the people, 10-powers to the states

Page 126 Answers:

1-19, 2-21, 3-26, 4-17, 5-15, 6-24, 7-12, 8-20, 9-18, 10-14, 11-25, 12-11, 13-13, 14-16, 15-22, 16-27, 17-23

Presidential Crossword Puzzle
Page 80 Answers:

ACROSS

1. BUSH
3. CARTER
9. GRANT
11. JACKSON
14. TAFT
16. MADISON
17. ADAMS
18. MCKINLEY
20. CLINTON
25. HARRISON
26. JEFFERSON
28. JOHNSON
29. WASHINGTON
30. CLEVELAND

DOWN

2. HOOVER
4. TRUMAN
5. REAGAN
6. WILSON
7. KENNEDY
8. OBAMA
10. TEDDY
12. NAPOLEON
13. NIXON
15. TRUMP
19. EISENHOWER
21. GARFIELD
22. LINCOLN
23. LBJ
24. FDR
27. FORD

ART AND PHOTOGRAPHY CREDITS

CPSIA information can be obtained
at www.ICGtesting.com
Printed in the USA
BVHW060008280921
617626BV00007B/124